AUTHORITY

and

SUBMISSION

WATCHMAN NEE

Living Stream Ministry
Anaheim, California • www.lsm.org

Second Edition, February 1998.

ISBN 0-7363-0185-2

Published by

Living Stream Ministry
2431 W. La Palma Ave., Anaheim, CA 92801 U.S.A.
P. O. Box 2121, Anaheim, CA 92814 U.S.A.

Printed in the United States of America

01 02 03 / 11 10 9 8 7 6 5 4 3

CONTENTS

PREFACE TO THE ENGLISH EDITION

In 1949 Watchman Nee released a series of messages on authority and submission in a co-workers' training held in Kuling, Foochow. All who were present in the meetings fell prostrate in the light of God. They had a deep sensation that the work of the unlawful one really fills the earth, while at the same time, the feeling of the Lord's saved ones is very insensitive. At the end of this age, how can the kingdom of God be brought in if the children of God do not bear a testimony for the Lord in submission?

In the last ten years some have edited these precious messages into outlines to be used as study material, and others have distributed copies of personal notes for study. Yet all of these are too brief and incomplete. Therefore, the Gospel Book Room gathered all of the available notes and edited them into eleven messages which were published in a series in *The Ministry of the Word* magazine last year. Because of the inadequacy of the notes, we feel that these messages as published are still short in content and deviate much from Brother Nee's original utterance and tone. As such, they can only be considered as the most detailed notes available. To meet the need of God's children in all the localities, we have put these eleven messages into this book with the hope that the Lord will make provisions for a more perfect record to be published in the future.

The Editors
Taiwan Gospel Book Room
January 20, 1967

PREFACE TO THE SECOND EDITION

Authority and Submission, based on a series of messages given by Watchman Nee in his training at Kuling Mountain in 1948 through 1949, contains two distinct but related parts. In 1988 the Living Stream Ministry published the first part under the title *Authority and Submission,* covering the general subject of spiritual authority and submission. This edition includes a second, previously untranslated, part covering the matter of being God's deputy authority.

PART ONE

AUTHORITY AND SUBMISSION

CHAPTER ONE

THE IMPORTANCE OF AUTHORITY

Scripture Reading: Rom. 13:1-7; Heb. 1:3; Isa. 14:12-14; Matt. 6:13; 26:62-64

THE THRONE OF GOD
ESTABLISHED UPON AUTHORITY

God's works issue from God's throne; God's throne is established upon authority. All things have been created by the authority of God, and all laws on earth are held together through authority. Hence, the Bible says that God upholds all things by the word, which is of His authority (Heb. 1:3b). It does not say that God upholds all things by His power. God's authority represents God Himself; God's power only represents God's works. It is easy to be forgiven of sin against God's power, but it is not that easy to be forgiven of sin against God's authority, because sinning against God's authority is sinning against God Himself. In the whole universe only God is authority. All other authorities are appointed by God. Nothing is greater than authority in the universe; nothing can surpass it. For this reason, if we want to serve God, we must know God's authority.

SATAN'S BEGINNING

Satan became Satan because he overstepped God's authority. He wanted to compete with God and to stand in opposition to God. Rebellion is the cause of the fall of Satan.

Both Isaiah 14:12-15 and Ezekiel 28:13-17 speak of the transgression and the fall of Satan. Isaiah 14 tells us that Satan violated God's authority, while Ezekiel 28 tells us that he violated God's holiness. Violating God's authority is a matter of rebellion; it is more serious than violating God's holiness. Sin is a matter of conduct; it is easy to be forgiven of sin. But rebellion is a matter of principle; it is not easy to be forgiven of rebellion. Satan, in trying to set up his throne above that of God's, violated God's authority. The principle of Satan is the principle of self-exaltation. Sin's coming into being was not the cause of Satan's fall. Rather, Satan's rebellion against God's authority, for which he was condemned by God, subsequently gave rise to sin.

Hence, if we want to serve God, we can never violate the matter of authority. To do so is to follow the principle of Satan. We can never preach the word of Christ under the principle of Satan. There is a possibility in God's work that we can stand in principle on Satan's side, while we stand in doctrine on Christ's side. All the while, we may think that we are still doing the Lord's work. This is a very evil thing. Satan is not afraid of us preaching the words of Christ. He is only afraid of us submitting to the authority of Christ. Our service to God can never be according to the principle of Satan. Once the principle of Christ comes, the principle of Satan has to go. Even now Satan is still a usurper in the air; he will not be cast out until the end of Revelation. Only when we wash ourselves spotlessly clean from the principle of Satan can we hope to serve God.

In the Lord's prayer in Matthew 6:9-13 there is the phrase, "And do not bring us into temptation." Temptation speaks of Satan's work. There is also the phrase, "But deliver us from the evil one." This refers to Satan himself. Following this, the Lord said, "For Yours is the kingdom and the power and the glory forever. Amen." This is the most important declaration. The kingdom is God's and so is the authority and the glory. Everything is God's. What sets us completely free from Satan is seeing this most precious thing—the kingdom is God's. The administration of the whole universe is under God. For this reason we have to learn to submit to God's authority. No one can steal God's glory.

Satan showed the Lord all the kingdoms of the earth, but the Lord said that all the kingdom of the heavens is God's. We need to see to whom authority ultimately belongs. When we preach the gospel we are bringing people under the authority of God. If we are to establish God's authority on earth, is it then possible for us not to meet authority ourselves? If we do not, how can we deal with Satan?

ALL DISPUTES IN THE UNIVERSE
BEING A MATTER OF AUTHORITY

The center of dispute in the whole universe relates to who has the authority. We have to contend with Satan by asserting that authority is with God. We have to set ourselves to submit to God's authority and to uphold God's authority. We must meet God's authority face-to-face and have a basic realization of it.

Before Paul realized authority, he wanted to eradicate the church from the earth. But after he met the Lord on the way to Damascus, he realized that it was difficult to kick against the goads (God's authority) with his feet (man's energy). He immediately fell down, acknowledged Jesus as Lord, and submitted to the instruction of Ananias in Damascus. Paul met God's authority. At his conversion, Paul was brought not only into a realization of God's salvation, but also into a realization of God's authority.

Paul was an intelligent and capable man, while Ananias was a very insignificant, small brother. The Bible refers to him only once. If Paul had not met God's authority, how could he possibly have listened to the words of Ananias? Unless a man meets authority on the way to "Damascus," he cannot submit to an insignificant, small brother in "Damascus." This shows us that anyone who has met authority will deal with the authority alone; he will not deal with the person involved. We should only think of the authority, not of the person, because our submission is not to a person but to God's authority in that person. If this is not our attitude, we do not know what authority is. If we deal with the person before submitting to authority, we are completely wrong. If we touch the matter of authority first and then submit to the person, irrespective of who he is, we are on the right path.

God has only one goal in the church, which is to manifest His authority in the universe. We can see God's authority from the coordination in the church.

God exercises the utmost of His strength to uphold His authority. His authority is stronger than anything else. We who are so self-confident, but who are in reality so blind, have to come face-to-face at least once with God's authority. Only when we are broken can we come into submission. Then we will begin to learn what God's authority is. Only when a man meets God's authority will he submit to the deputy authority whom God appoints.

THE GREATEST DEMAND IN THE BIBLE
BEING SUBMISSION TO GOD'S WILL

The greatest demand God has on man is not bearing the cross, offerings, consecration, or self-sacrifice. God's greatest demand on man is submission. God commanded Saul to smite the Amalekites and utterly destroy all that they had (1 Sam. 15:1-3). But after Saul overcame the Amalekites, he spared Agag the king of Amalek. He also appreciated the best sheep, the best oxen, and all that was good and refused to destroy them, hoping instead to offer them as sacrifices to God (vv. 7-9, 14-15). But Samuel said to him, "To obey is better than sacrifice, / And to heed, than the fat of rams" (v. 22). The sacrifice spoken of here is the burnt offering; it has nothing to do with sin. It is for God's acceptance and satisfaction. However, Samuel said that to heed and to obey are better than sacrifice. This is because even in this kind of sacrifice there was the possibility of a mixture with the self-will. Only in heeding and obeying is there an absolute honoring of God and an exaltation of His will.

Obedience is the other end of authority. In order to have obedience, one must first keep the self out of the picture. One must not try to obey with the self. There the possibility of obedience only by living in the spirit. Obedience is the highest expression of response to God's will.

THE LORD'S PRAYER
IN THE GARDEN OF GETHSEMANE

Some have considered the Lord's prayer in the garden of Gethsemane, where His sweat fell as blood, as a sign of His weakness in the flesh and His fear of the cup (Luke 22:44).

But this is not true. The prayer in Gethsemane is the same in principle as what is recorded in 1 Samuel 15:22. The Lord's prayer in Gethsemane is the highest expression of submission to God's authority. Our Lord's submission to God's authority far exceeds His sacrifice on the cross. He earnestly sought to know God's will. He did not say, "I will take the cross" or "I must drink the cup." He only heeded and obeyed. He said, "If it is possible, let this cup pass from Me" (Matt. 26:39b). Here His own preference is not seen, because following this, He said, "Yet not as I will, but as You will" (v. 39c). God's will is absolute, but the cup (i.e., the cross) is not. If it had not been God's will for Him to be crucified, the Lord Jesus very well could have disregarded the cross. Before the Lord was clear concerning God's will, the "cup" and "God's will" were two different things. But after He was clear, the "cup" became the "cup" that the Father had given to Him, and it and God's will became one thing. A will is the representative of an authority. Hence, when submission comes from knowing God's will, that submission is a submission to authority. If there is no prayer and no willingness to know God's will, how can there be submission to authority?

Again the Lord said, "The cup which the Father has given Me, shall I not drink it?" (John 18:11). Here the Lord was upholding the authority of God. The Lord was not upholding His own cross. At the same time, when He understood that drinking the cup (i.e., being crucified for our redemption) was the will of God, He immediately said, "Arise, let us be going" (Matt. 26:46). He promptly obeyed. Since the cross means the accomplishment of God's will, the Lord's death is the highest expression of submission to authority. Although the cross is the center of the whole universe, it is not higher than the will of God. The Lord upholds the authority of God (the will) more than He upholds His own cross (the sacrifice).

Our service to God is not a matter of voluntary sacrifice or of denial of our self. It is a matter of accomplishing God's will. It is not a matter of picking up the cross. Rather, it is the submission to God's will. This is the basic principle. If the principle of rebellion is present, even a sacrifice is an enjoyment and a glory to Satan. Saul could offer up sheep and oxen, but God would not recognize that as a sacrifice because the principle of Satan was present. To overturn God's authority is to overturn God. Hence, the Bible says that rebellion is like the sin of divination, and insubordination is like idolatry and teraphim (1 Sam. 15:23).

We who are involved in the Lord's work are the servants of God. As such, the first thing we touch is the matter of authority. Touching authority is as real as the matter of touching salvation. For us this is a deeper lesson. We must be touched and smitten at least once by authority. Only then can we work the work of God. In our relationship with God, nothing is more important than touching authority. Once we touch it, we will see it wherever we turn. Only then can we be restricted by God, and only then can we begin to be used by God.

THE JUDGMENT OF THE LORD AND OF PAUL

In Matthew 26 and 27 the Lord was summoned for two kinds of judgment: from religion before the high priest (26:57-66) and from the civil government before Pilate (27:11-14). When interrogated by Pilate, the Lord could choose not to answer, because He was not bound by earthly rule. But when the high priest adjured Him by the name of the living God, the Lord had to answer. This is a question of submission to authority. Again in Acts 23 when Paul was judged, after he realized that Ananias was the high priest of God, he readily submitted. We who are workers of the Lord must come face-to-face with this matter of authority. Otherwise, our work will not be in the principle of God's will, which is the principle of submission to authority. Instead, we will be in the principle of Satan's rebellion, which is the principle of working without God's will. This matter indeed requires a great revelation.

In Matthew 7:21-23 the Lord rebuked those who prophesied, cast out demons, and performed many wonderful works in His name. What was wrong with this work in the Lord's name? It was wrong because man was the source in all these works. Out of themselves men were working in the name of the Lord. This was the activity of the flesh. For this reason the Lord considered it to be lawlessness. Their work could not be considered as work. Following this word, the Lord said that only those who do the Father's will can enter the kingdom of the heavens. This shows that all works should originate from submission to God's will. God has to be the source. All works are assigned by God. No work should be sought out by man. Only when a man understands God's will in His assignment can there be the experience of the reality of the authority of the kingdom of the heavens.

THE REALIZATION OF AUTHORITY BEING A GREAT REVELATION

In the universe there are two great things: believing unto salvation and submitting to authority. In other words, to trust and obey. The Bible shows us that the definition of sin is lawlessness (1 John 3:4). In Romans 2:12 the phrase "without the law" is the same as "lawless." To be lawless is to disregard the authority of God, and to disregard the authority of God is sin. To transgress is a matter of conduct, but to be lawless is a matter of attitude and heart. The present age is one of lawlessness; the world is full of sins of lawlessness. Even the lawless one is about to be manifested. At the same time, authority will have less and less place in the world. In the end all authority will be overthrown. What remains will be a reign of lawlessness.

Hence, there are two principles in the universe—God's authority and Satan's rebellion. We cannot serve God on the one hand, while taking the way of rebellion with a spirit of rebellion on the other hand. Although a rebellious person can preach, Satan will laugh, because the principle of Satan is there in the preaching. Service is ever attendant to authority. Do we want to submit to God's authority or not? We who serve God must gain this basic understanding at some time. It is like touching electricity. Once one touches it, he will never be careless with it. In the same way, once a man meets God's authority and is smitten by it, his eyes will be enlightened. He will be able to discern not only himself, but others as well. He will know who is and who is not lawless.

May God be merciful to us that we would be delivered from the way of rebellion. We can lead God's children in the proper path only when we know God's authority and have learned the lesson of submission.

CHAPTER TWO

EXAMPLES OF REBELLION IN THE OLD TESTAMENT

(1)

Scripture Reading: Gen. 2:16-17; 3:1-6; Rom. 5:19

THE FALL OF ADAM AND EVE

The Fall of Man Due to Not Submitting

Let us consider the story of Adam and Eve in Genesis 2 and 3. After Adam was created, God gave him some instructions. He commanded Adam not to eat of the fruit of the tree of the knowledge of good and evil. We must realize that this was not merely a matter of eating or not eating the forbidden fruit. Rather, God put Adam under a kind of authority with a view that Adam would submit to it. God entrusted all creation to Adam's authority so that Adam would manage and be the authority over all the creation. At the same time, God put Adam under His own authority so that Adam would learn to submit to authority. Only those who submit to authority can themselves be authorities.

In the order of God's creation, He first created Adam and then Eve. God destined that Adam would be the authority and that Eve would be under Adam's authority. God set one to be the authority and the other to submit. In the old creation and in the new creation, the order of precedence is the basis of authority. Whoever is created first is the authority. Whoever is saved first is the authority. For this reason, wherever we go, our first thought should be to find those to whom the Lord wants us to submit. Wherever we are, we have to see authority, and we also have to submit to authority.

Man's fall came from not submitting to authority. Eve did not check with Adam; she made the decision. She saw that the fruit was good for food and pleasant to the eyes, so she took liberty and made the decision herself. Before she stretched forth her hand to pick the fruit, she first used her head to think and receive the temptation. Then she assumed the headship by stretching forth her hands. Hence, the taking of the fruit by Eve did not come from submission. Rather, it came from the decision of the self. Not only did she transgress God's commandment, she also disregarded Adam's authority. Rebellion against God's deputy authority is rebellion against God Himself. Adam listened to Eve's word and took of the fruit. This was worse; it was in disobedience to God's direct command. As a result, Adam also disregarded God's authority and was rebellious.

All Work Needing to Be Done out of Submission

While we live on this earth, our first question should not be whether or not we should do a certain thing. Rather, in doing a certain thing, we should ask to whom are we submitting. It is not a matter of doing or not doing. It is a matter of to whom we submit. Without submission there is no work and there is no service. When Adam took the fruit, the first question that should have been asked was whether or not this was in submission to God. All of the work of a Christian should come out of submission. Nothing is of our own initiative; everything is responsive. No act is active; everything is passive. In other words, everything should be initiated by God; nothing should be initiated by us.

Not only was Eve under the authority of God; she was also under the authority that God had set—Adam. Eve had to submit to a double command and a double authority. This is the same for us today. Eve only thought of the fruit being good for food. She did not know to whom she should submit in eating. From the very beginning, God wanted man to submit rather than to propose his own ideas. Eve's act, however, originated from her own idea, not from submission. She neither submitted to God's arrangement nor to God's authority. Instead, she proposed her own idea, transgressed against God, and became fallen. To fall is to act without submission. An act that has no submission behind it is rebellion.

The more submission a man has, the less acts there are with him. At the beginning of a man's pursuit after the Lord, there are many acts and little submission. As he progresses, the acts become fewer, until in the end only submission is left. When many encounter work, they like to take action. They do not like to be still. They do not care whether or not there is submission. For this reason, many works are done by the self, not through heeding and obedience.

Right and Wrong Are in God

Man should not do anything out of a knowledge of right and wrong. Rather, he should do all things out of obedience. The principle of discerning good and evil is the principle of living by right and wrong. Before Adam and Eve took the fruit, their right and wrong were in God. If they did not live before God, they knew nothing; both their right and wrong were just God Himself. But after man received of the tree of the knowledge of good and evil, he found a source of discerning between right and wrong apart from God. As a consequence, after man's fall, there was no need for him to seek after God. He could get along by himself. He could isolate himself from God and judge between right and wrong. This is the fall. The work of redemption enables us to turn back to God for our right and wrong.

Christians Needing to Submit to Authority

All authority is from God because everything is ordered by God. If we trace any authority upward, we eventually will come to God. God is above all authorities, and every authority is under Him. Once we touch God's authority, we touch God Himself. Basically, God's work is not carried out by power, but by authority. He upholds everything by the word, which is of His authority. Creation came about through the word of His authority. His word is His authority. We do not know how God's authority works. But we know that God accomplishes everything through His authority.

The centurion whose servant was sick knew that there was an authority above him to which he should submit, inasmuch as there were those under him who submitted to him. Therefore, he only needed the Lord to say one word, and he believed that the matter would then be taken care of. He knew that all authority was in the Lord's hand; he believed in the Lord's authority. This is why the Lord said that He had found no faith greater than this. Meeting God's authority is the same as meeting God. Today God appoints authorities everywhere in the universe. All the orbits in the universe are established by Him; all the ways in the world are set up by Him. Hence, they are all under His authority. Offending God's authority is the same as offending God Himself. A Christian should submit to authority.

The First Lesson for a Worker
Being to Submit to Authority

Our position is to be under others' authority on the one hand, while having others under our authority on the other hand. Other than God Himself, everyone, including the Lord Jesus, has to submit to authority on earth. We should see authority everywhere. Both at home and in school there are authorities. When you see a policeman on the street, even though you may know that he is incapable and that his learning is not as high as yours, you have to consider him as God's appointed authority. When a few brothers are together, they should know how to line themselves up immediately. Everyone should know where he stands. A worker should know who is his authority. Some never realize who their authority is. They have never submitted to anyone. With us there should never be right or wrong, good or evil. Wherever we go, we should first know who is the authority. If you know who you have to submit to, you will spontaneously know what position you should occupy in the Body, and you will stand in your proper position. But there are many Christians today in whom there is not even a thought about submission. For them everything is confused; with them there is no such thing as keeping one's position. Submission is the first lesson for those who work. It is actually the major part of their work.

The Need to Recover Submission

When Adam fell, the order in the universe was destroyed. We should never try to differentiate between good and evil. Rather, we should submit to authority. Man is prone to judge good and evil by himself. He feels that this is good and that is not good. It seems as if man's judgment is clearer than God's. This, however, is a condition of foolishness and the fall. This must be removed from us, for this is nothing but rebellion.

The scant submission that we see now is not enough. Some think that it is enough to be baptized and forsake the denominations. But this is not enough. There are many young students who think that God is chastising them by requiring them to submit to their teachers. There are many wives who think that God is chastising them by requiring them to submit to a husband who is impossible to live under. There are many Christians who are still living in rebellion. They have not learned even the basic step in submission.

Submission in the Bible is submission to God's appointed authority. How shallow is the submission which has been preached hitherto! Submission is the basic principle. If the matter of authority is not solved, nothing can be done well. Faith is the principle by which we receive life, while submission is the principle by which we conduct our living. All of the divisions and denominations of the church today come from rebellion. In order to restore authority, submission must be restored first. Many are accustomed to acting as the head; they have never known submission. But we must learn submission. It must become our reaction.

God has not hidden one thing from us concerning authority. In the church, whether directly or indirectly, God has shown us how to submit to authority. Many only know about submission to God; they do not know about submission to authorities. Because all authorities are from God, everyone has to submit to authority. All of man's problems are due to living outside the realm of God's authority.

No Oneness of the Body
without the Authority of the Head

Today God is taking the way of the recovery of the oneness of the Body of Christ. In order to have the oneness of the Body, there must first be the life of the Head and then the authority of the Head. Without the life of the Head, there is no Body. Likewise, without the authority of the Head, there is no oneness of the Body. We must allow the life of the Head to rule so that the Body can become one. God requires that we submit not only to Him, but also to all His deputy authorities. All the members have to learn to submit to one another. The Body is one. The Head and the Body are also one. God's will can be accomplished only when the authority of the Head prevails. God wants the church be the kingdom of God.

A Few Points on the Lesson
of Submission to Authority

A servant of God will eventually encounter authority in the universe, in his community, in his home, or in the church. If a man has never met God's authority, how can he submit to God? This is not a matter of doctrine or teaching. If it is, it will still be abstract to us. Some think that submission to authority is a very difficult thing. But it is not difficult when one meets God. Unless God's mercy is upon us, no one can submit to God's authority. For this reason, there should be a few points for us to learn:

(1) There must be a spirit of submission.

(2) There must be the training in submission. Some people are like savages; they cannot come under any submission. We have appointed a housekeeper for every household with the hope that we would all learn submission. [Translator's Note: This refers to the dormitories of the training in which these messages were delivered.] Everyone should receive training by standing in the proper position. One who has learned the lesson or who has been trained will not feel restricted no

matter where he is placed. He will spontaneously live out submission without any difficulty.

(3) One must learn to be a deputy authority. A worker of God must not only learn submission to authority; he must also learn to be God's deputy authority in the church and in the home. If God entrusts him with many things, and if he has learned to submit under God's authority, he will not feel boastful about anything. However, some who have learned to submit to others find that they do not know how to be the authority when they are brought by God to a place to work. Therefore, not only do we have to learn to submit to authority, but we also have to learn to be the authority and to stand in the proper position. On the one hand, the church suffers because many do not submit. On the other hand, the church suffers because many do not know how to be the authority by standing in the proper position.

CHAPTER THREE

EXAMPLES OF REBELLION IN THE OLD TESTAMENT

(2)

Scripture Reading: Gen. 9:20-27; Lev. 10:1-2; Num. 12:1-15; 16

THE REBELLION OF HAM

The Failure of the Deputy Authority Being a Test to Those Submitting to Authority

In the first garden, Adam fell. In the second garden, Noah also fell. God saved Noah's household because of his righteousness. In God's plan, Noah was the head of his household. God placed Noah's family under his authority. God also set Noah to be the head of the earth at that time.

But one day Noah drank of the wine of the vineyard and became drunk. He became naked in the tent. When his son Ham saw his father's nakedness, he went out and told his two brothers. As far as his conduct was concerned, Noah was wrong; he should not have been drunk. But Ham did not see the seriousness of authority. The father is the authority set up by God in the family. However, the flesh loves to see authority exposed to shame so that there can be freedom from restriction. When Ham saw the impropriety of his father, there was no sense of shame or sorrow. He also did not think of covering the matter. This proves that he had a spirit of rebellion. He went out to tell his brothers and expose the shame of his father. This proves that he also had a reviling conduct. But notice how Shem and Japheth dealt with the matter. They went into the tent backward. They did not turn their faces toward their father's shame; instead, they covered their father with the garment on their shoulders. The failure of Noah became a test to Shem, Ham, Japheth, and Canaan the son of Ham. It showed who was submissive and who was rebellious. Noah's failure exposed Ham's rebellion.

When Noah woke up from his drunkenness, he prophesied that the descendant of Ham would be cursed and that he would be a servant of servants to his brothers. The first slave in the Bible is Ham. The phrase "Canaan shall be his servant" is used twice. This means that those who do not submit to authority will have to be slaves, being subject to authority. Shem was blessed. The Lord Jesus was born of the descendants of Shem. Those of Japheth are the preachers of Christ. All the nations that preach the gospel are descendants of Japheth. After the flood, the first person who was cursed was Ham. His descendants were made to be slaves under others' authority for generation after generation. Everyone who learns to serve the Lord must come face-to-face with authority. He cannot serve God in a spirit of lawlessness.

NADAB AND ABIHU OFFERING STRANGE FIRE

The Reason for Devouring

How solemn is the story of Nadab and Abihu! They became priests because they belonged to the house of Aaron. This was due to the proper condition of their house before God; it was not due to the proper condition of the individuals in that house. God appointed Aaron to be the priest. The anointing was upon the head of Aaron (Lev. 8:12). In all things related to offerings and service, the chief person was Aaron. His sons were just helpers taking orders from him to attend to the affairs beside the altar. God had no intention for Aaron's sons to be priests independently. He only wanted them to be under Aaron's authority. Leviticus 8 refers to Aaron and his sons twelve times. Then chapter nine indicates that Aaron offered the sacrifices while his sons helped alongside of him. If Aaron did not move, his sons should not have moved. Everything should have been under Aaron's name. Nothing should have been under his sons' names. When his sons assumed the headship presumptuously to offer sacrifices, it became strange fire. But the sons of Aaron, Nadab and Abihu, thought that they also could offer sacrifices. Without Aaron's command, they offered up strange fire. The meaning of strange fire is to serve God while refusing to take orders and disregarding authority. They observed that it was a simple matter for their father to offer sacrifices. Nothing extraordinary seemed to be involved; therefore, they thought that they could do the same. Hence, they took the matter into their own hands. Their only consideration was whether or not the matter could be done. They did not consider the matter of God's authority.

Service Originating from God

Here we see a very solemn matter. Serving God and offering strange fire are two similar matters, yet they are very different. Service to God originates from God. It is man serving God through submission to His authority. The result is acceptance. Strange fire, however, originates from man. There is no need of obedience to God's will or submission to His authority. All that is needed is man's zeal, and the result is death. We often incur more death the more we serve and work. Under such circumstances we have to ask God to enlighten us. Are we under the principle of service, or are we under the principle of strange fire?

God's Work Being a Coordination in Authority

When Nadab and Abihu worked apart from Aaron, they were working apart from God, because God's work is a coordination in authority. God ordained that they serve under Aaron's authority. In the New Testament there are Barnabas and Paul, Paul and Timothy, and Peter and Mark. In all these we see a responsible one who leads on the one hand and a helper who follows on the other hand. In God's work some are set to be authorities while others are set to submit to authorities. God desires that we be priests according to the order of Melchisedec. In the same way, we have to serve God in the order of the coordination in authority.

When a person who should not take the lead begins to take the lead, there is rebellion and death. Therefore, anyone who serves God without touching authority is offering strange fire. If someone says, "Since So-and-so can do it, I can do the same," this is rebellion. God pays attention not only to whether or not there is fire, but also to the nature of the fire. Rebellion can change the nature of fire. All that is not instructed by Aaron, that is, not instructed by God, is strange fire. God's concern is with the upholding of authority, not just the sacrifice. For this reason, man should be a follower. He should always be a complementing one. A deputy authority follows God. Those who submit to authority follow the deputy authorities. In spiritual matters or spiritual works it is not an individual serving, but a corporate Body coordinating in serving. The unit of service is coordination, not individuals. When Nadab and Abihu got into trouble with Aaron, they got into trouble with God. They could not work apart from Aaron. Anyone who violates authority will be devoured by the fire of God. Even Aaron himself did not know that the matter was so serious, but Moses knew the solemnness of rebelling against God's authority. There are many who think that they are serving God. Yet they work independently without coming under any authority. Many have sinned without realizing that they are rebelling against God's authority. For this reason, the free-lance evangelists who were prevalent in China in the past were a great loss to the church.

THE REVILING OF AARON AND MIRIAM

Incurring God's Anger
by Reviling the Deputy Authority

Aaron and Miriam were the older brother and sister of Moses. In the family Moses was under the authority of Aaron and Miriam. But in God's calling and work, Aaron and Miriam were under Moses' authority. They were not happy about Moses marrying an Ethiopian woman, and they spoke against and reviled Moses, saying, "Has Jehovah indeed spoken only through Moses? Has he not spoken through us also?" (Num. 12:2). Ethiopians are Africans. They are the descendants of Ham. It was not right for Moses to marry an Ethiopian. Miriam was older than Moses. It was all right for her to rebuke her brother on the ground of family relationship. But in opening her mouth, she touched the work of God and overstepped Moses' position. In His work, God had placed deputy authority in the hand of Moses. It was a big mistake for Miriam and Aaron to speak against Moses because of family problems.

God appointed Moses to lead the Israelites out of Egypt. But Miriam despised Moses. For this reason, God was not happy with her. It is all right for you to deal with your brother. But it is not all right for you to speak against God's authority. Neither Aaron nor Miriam knew God's authority. They fostered a rebellious heart by standing on natural ground. Moses did not answer. He knew that if he was God's appointed authority, there was no need for anyone to protect him. Whoever spoke against him would touch death. He did not need to open his mouth. As long as God had given him authority, he did not have to speak. A lion does not need protection because it is the authority. Moses first submitted to God's authority. Then he was able to represent God as authority. He was very meek, more than all men who were on the face of the earth (v. 3). The authority which Moses represented was the authority of God. All authorities are delegated by God, and no one can take them away.

Their words of rebellion ascended upward and were heard by God (v. 2b). When Aaron and Miriam offended Moses, they offended God in Moses. Therefore, God became angry. Once a man touches deputy authority, he touches God in that person. Once he offends the delegated authority, he offends God.

Authority Being God's Selection
Rather than Man's Attainment

God called all three to come out to the entrance of the tent of meeting (v. 4). Aaron and Miriam came out boldly, presuming that they would be vindicated. They thought that God had finally called them. They thought, "You, Moses, have married an Ethiopian woman and have caused unhappiness in the family. We have many things to say to God." But God said, "Moses is My servant. He is faithful in all My house. Why are you so bold as to speak against My servant?" Spiritual authority does not come through man's attainment.

Rather, it comes through God's selection. Spiritual matters are entirely different from worldly principles. Authority is God Himself. It cannot be offended. Whoever speaks against Moses speaks against God's selection. We cannot despise God's selection.

The Manifestation of Rebellion Being Leprosy

When the anger of God was kindled, the cloud removed from over the tent, and the presence of God was gone. Immediately, Miriam became leprous (v. 10). This was not from infection. It was inflicted by God. Being leprous is not any better than marrying an Ethiopian woman. As soon as inward rebellion is manifested, it becomes leprosy. Lepers have to be shut out. Man cannot approach them. They lose all fellowship.

When Aaron saw that Miriam became leprous, he besought Moses to be a mediator so that God would heal her. God instructed Miriam to be shut out from the camp seven days before she could be received again. She bore shame for seven days as if her father had spit in her face. Only after seven days did the tent of meeting journey on. Whenever there is rebellion and reviling among us, God's presence is gone, and the tent will not move. The pillar of cloud will not come until reviling words have been judged. If the matter of authority is not settled, all other matters will remain unsettled.

Submitting to God's Direct Authority and Also Submitting to His Deputy Authority

Many think that they have submitted themselves to God already. They do not know that they still need to submit to God's deputy authority. Those who are truly submissive see God's authority in all environments—in their homes and in all institutions. God said, "Why then were you not afraid to speak against My servant, against Moses?" (v. 8). Every time reviling words come, we have to pay much attention to them. We cannot be careless, thinking that we can say things rashly. When there is reviling, it proves that there is the spirit of rebellion within. The reviling is the sprouting of this rebellion. We have to fear God and must not speak in a rash way.

Many today speak against those ahead of them. They speak against the responsible brothers in the church, but they do not realize the seriousness of this matter. If one day the church receives grace from God, she will separate herself from those who revile the servant of God. She will not talk to them because they are leprous. May God be merciful to us that we would see that this is not a matter with our brother, but a matter of God's appointed authority. If we have met authority, we will realize that there are too many incidents where we sin against God. Thereafter, our concept concerning sin will be changed. We will see sin from God's point of view. The sin that God condemns is man's rebellion.

THE REBELLION OF KORAH'S COMPANY, AND OF DATHAN AND ABIRAM

A Corporate Rebellion

Numbers 16 speaks of the company of Korah, who were Levites, and Dathan and Abiram, who were of the tribe of Reuben. The Levites represented the tribe of spirituality; Dathan and Abiram represented the leaders. In addition, there were two hundred fifty well-known men. All of these princes gathered together to rebel. They attacked Moses and Aaron, saying, "You have gone too far! For all the assembly is holy....Why then do you exalt yourselves above the congregation of Jehovah?" (v. 3). They did not respect Moses and Aaron. Perhaps they spoke these words in all honesty. They did not see the authority of Jehovah. They thought that this was a personal matter. They considered that among God's people there was no authority. When they rebuked Moses, they mentioned nothing about Moses' relationship with God or God's command in this matter. When Moses heard these serious charges, he was neither angry nor upset. Instead, he fell before Jehovah. He did not act in any way by himself. He did not try to exercise authority, because authority is of God. He told the company of Korah to wait until the morning. In the morning Jehovah would prove who was His and who was holy. He was answering an improper spirit with a proper spirit.

The words of Korah's company were based completely on reasonings. Their words were entirely suppositions. But Moses said that the Lord would make everything clear. It was all a matter of Jehovah's selection and command. It was not Moses' problem but Jehovah's problem. They thought that they were only against Moses and Aaron, that they were not against God. They had no intention of rebelling against God. They intended to continue to serve God. They were only despising Moses and Aaron. But God cannot be separated from His deputy authority. One cannot take one attitude towards God and a different attitude towards Moses and Aaron. No one can reject God's deputy authority on the one hand while receiving God on the other hand. If they had submitted to the authority of Moses and Aaron, they would have been submitting to God. But Moses did not lift himself up because of God's authority on him. He humbled himself under the authority of God. In a gentle way he said to them, "Take censers,...and put fire in them and place incense upon them before Jehovah tomorrow, and the man whom Jehovah chooses, he shall be holy" (vv. 6-7). Moses was an aged man. He knew the consequence of such an act, and he sighed, saying, "You have gone too far, sons of Levi!...Is it too small a thing for you that the God of Israel has separated you from the assembly of Israel to bring you near to Himself?...Therefore you and all your company have gathered together against Jehovah" (vv. 7, 9, 11).

At that time Dathan and Abiram were not present. Later Moses sent men to ask them to come. But they refused, saying, "You have not brought us into a land flowing with milk and honey, nor given us an inheritance of fields and vineyards. Will you put out the eyes of these men? We will not come up" (v. 14). Their attitude was that of rebellion. Basically, they did not believe in the promise of God. Their attention was on the earthly blessing. They forgot their own mistake—they were the ones who had refused to enter Canaan. But they turned around to rebel against Moses with bitter words.

God Must Remove Rebellion from among His People

Then Moses became angry. He did not answer them, but

prayed to God instead. Many times man's rebellion forces God
to step forth in judgment. The Israelites tempted God ten
times and doubted Him five times. But God tolerated and
forgave all of them. Yet when rebellion broke out this time,
God stepped forth to judge. He said, "Separate yourselves
from among this assembly that I may consume them in a
moment" (v. 21). God must remove rebellion from among His
people. Moses and Aaron fell down before God and prayed,
"Shall one man sin, and will You be angry with all the
assembly?" (v. 22). God answered Moses and Aaron's prayer
and judged only the company of Korah. Not only did the
Israelites have to hearken to God's appointed authority, but
God Himself also testified before the Israelites that He
accepted their word.

Rebellion is a principle from Hades. When they rebelled,
the gates of Hades were opened. The earth opened its mouth
and swallowed Korah, Dathan, Abiram, their households, and
all their goods. They fell into Hades alive. The gates of Hades
cannot prevail against the church. But a spirit of rebellion
can open the gates. The church is not victorious because there
are rebellious ones within her. When there is no rebellion,
the earth cannot open its mouth. All kinds of sins release
death. Only submission to authority will shut the gates of
Hades and release life.

Submissive Ones Acting
Not by Doctrine but by Faith

When the rebellious ones spoke against Moses for not
leading them into the land flowing with milk and honey, and
for not giving them the inheritance of fields and vineyards,
their words were somewhat true. They were then in the
wilderness and were, indeed, not yet in the land flowing with
milk and honey. Please note that whenever men act and judge
according to doctrine or according to what they see with their
physical eyes, they are taking the way of reason. But those
who submit to authority will enter Canaan by faith. The way
of the spirit can never be taken by those who argue and
reason. Those who by faith take the leading of the pillars of
cloud and of fire and take the leading of Moses, the deputy

authority, will enjoy the fullness of the Spirit. The earth opens its mouth for the rebellious ones. This is the way of death leading them quickly to Hades. Those who do not submit to authority have clear eyes, but they only see the desolation in the wilderness. Only those who are apparently blind, who probe forward by faith, ignoring the present desolation, can enter into Canaan. Those on the spiritual pathway see the future promise of blessing by the eyes of faith. Therefore, one must meet authority, be restricted by God, and be led by His deputy authority. If a man sees only his father, brothers, or sisters, he does not know what authority is, and has not yet met God. In any case, the matter of authority is an inward revelation rather than an outward teaching.

The Contagion of Rebellion

In Numbers 16 there are two rebellions. In verses 1 through 40 we have the rebellion of the leaders, whereas in verses 41 through 50 we have the rebellion of the whole assembly. A spirit of rebellion is contagious. The judgment on the two hundred fifty was not enough to warn the whole assembly. They saw with their own eyes fire coming forth from God to consume the two hundred fifty incense burners. Yet they still rebelled. They even accused Moses of killing them. Moses and Aaron could not open the earth; it was God who opened it. Moses could not consume people with fire; it was the fire that proceeded from Jehovah God that judged the people. Some men only see through their own eyes. They do not see that all authority is of God. Such people are very bold; they are not afraid even when they see judgment, because they do not have the knowledge of authority. This is a very dangerous matter. When the whole assembly attacked Moses and Aaron, the glory of God appeared, proving that authority is from God. God came forth to judge. A plague broke out, and 14,700 died. Moses was quick in his spiritual sensation; he immediately ordered Aaron to take the censer, put fire in it, and place incense on it to make propitiation for the assembly. Aaron stood between the dead and the living, and the plague was stopped.

God can bear His people's ten murmurings in the wilderness. But He cannot bear His authority being offended. God can bear many sins and can even pardon them. Once rebellion appears, however, God cannot tolerate it, for rebellion is according to the principle of death. It is according to the principle of Satan. For this reason, the sin of rebellion is more serious than any other kind of sin. Whenever someone opposes authority, God immediately comes in to judge. How solemn a matter this is!

CHAPTER FOUR

DAVID'S KNOWLEDGE OF AUTHORITY

Scripture Reading: 1 Sam. 24:4-6; 26:9, 11; 2 Sam. 1:14

DAVID GAINING THE THRONE
WITHOUT PAYING THE PRICE OF REBELLION

During the setting up of the kingdom of Israel, God officially established His authority on earth. When the Israelites entered Canaan they asked God for a king, and God sent Samuel to anoint Saul as their first king (1 Sam. 10:1). Saul was chosen by God. God set him up as the authority, that is, as His deputy authority. But when he became king, Saul did not submit to the authority of God. He violated God's authority. In refusing to kill the king of Amalek and the best of the sheep and oxen, he rebelled against God and disobeyed His words. Therefore, God set Saul aside and anointed David (1 Sam. 15—16). However, David was under Saul's authority. He was one of Saul's subjects and was even a soldier in Saul's camp. Later, he even became Saul's son-in-law. Both of these men had the anointing upon them. But Saul often sought to kill David. There were two kings in Israel. One was set aside but still sitting on the throne. The other was chosen but not inaugurated. At this juncture David was in a very difficult situation.

In 1 Samuel 24 we see Saul chasing David in the wilderness of Engedi. When Saul went into a cave to cover his feet, David and his followers were in the innermost part of the cave. His followers suggested that David kill Saul, but David rejected the temptation. He dared not rebel against authority with his own hands (vv. 1-7). David was anointed by God. Concerning the throne, he stood in the proper position of God's plan and will. Who would have had anything to say about him being king? What would be wrong if David helped himself become king? Would it not be a good way to help God to accomplish His will? But David deeply felt that this could not be done. If he had killed Saul, it would have been in the principle of rebellion against God's authority, because God's anointing was still upon Saul. Although Saul was rejected, he was still God's anointed and still set up by God. If he had killed Saul, David could have become king immediately, and God's will would not have been delayed. But David was a man that denied his self. He would rather see his kingship postponed and God's plan delayed than to become a rebellious one. As a result he was eventually made God's authority.

At one time God set Saul to be king and David was under Saul's authority. If David had killed Saul, he would have gained the kingship at the price of rebellion. He would have fallen on the ground of rebellion. David dared not do this. This is the same in principle as Michael not daring to bring a reviling judgment against Satan (Jude 9). Authority is a tremendous matter.

SUBMISSION BEING HIGHER THAN OUR WORK

If a man is to serve God, he must submit to authority. Submission is higher than our work. Even if David set the whole kingdom in order, this would avail nothing without being under God's authority; he would still be like Saul. In the Old Testament Saul loved the best of the sheep and the oxen and would not destroy them, but rather saved them for offering. This is in the same principle of rebellion as Judas in the New Testament, who betrayed the Lord Jesus out of his love for thirty pieces of silver (Matt. 26:14-16). Offerings cannot cover up rebellion. If David wanted to accomplish God's will and plan, he could have killed Saul. Then he could have served God right away. But David dared not do this. He waited for God to work. He was willing to be submissive. David only cut off the skirt of Saul's cloak, and even then his heart smote him. His feeling was as sensitive as a New Testament believer. What we condemn is not just murder; even the cutting off of another's garment with a little knife is wrong and is rebellion. Backbiting, an evil eye, or a grudge in the heart may not be murder, but they are similar to the cutting off of another's garment, and they proceed from a spirit of rebellion.

David was one who knew God's authority from his heart. He was chased by Saul many times, yet he still submitted to God's authority. He considered Saul as lord, the anointed of Jehovah. This speaks of an important matter. Submission to authority is not submission to a person. It is submission to the anointing upon the person, the anointing which was upon him when God set him up as authority. David knew of the anointing on Saul. He acknowledged that Saul was God's anointed. Hence, he could only seek for his own escape; he could not put forth his hand to hurt Saul. Saul was disobedient to God's command. He was rejected by God. But this was something between Saul and God. As for David, he submitted to God's anointed. This was David's responsibility before God.

DAVID UPHOLDING GOD'S AUTHORITY
IN AN ABSOLUTE WAY

God wants His authority to be upheld in an absolute way. He has to recover this matter. Look again into 1 Samuel 26. A similar thing happened in the wilderness of Ziph. A second temptation came. Saul fell asleep, and David came into the place where he slept. Abishai wanted to kill Saul, but David forbade him. He swore and said, "Who can stretch forth his hand against Jehovah's anointed and be guiltless?" This is the second time that David spared Saul. He only took Saul's spear and water jug (vv. 7-12). This was an improvement from the previous time. He did not take anything from Saul's body. Instead, he only took something from beside his body. He gave up the chance of saving his own life to submit to and uphold God's authority.

According to 1 Samuel 31 and 2 Samuel 1, Saul killed himself. A young Amalekite came to David to claim the credit, saying that he had killed Saul. David's attitude was still that of denying the self and submitting to God's authority. He said to the man, "How is it that you were not afraid to stretch forth your hand to destroy Jehovah's anointed?" (2 Sam. 1:14). Then he ordered that the young messenger be killed.

Because David maintained God's authority, he was called a man after God's heart. His kingdom has been preserved until now, for the Lord is a descendant of David. Only those who submit to authority can themselves be the authority. This is a serious matter. We must uproot rebellion from among us. In order to be an authority, there must first be submission to authority. This one matter is crucial. Apart from this, we have no way to go on. The church is an organ of submission. There is no need to fear the weak ones in the church; there is only the need to fear the rebellious ones. We must submit to God's authority from our heart. Only then will the church be blessed. The way ahead depends on us. We are here to spend our days in a sober way.

CHAPTER FIVE

THE SON'S SUBMISSION

Scripture Reading: Phil. 2:5-11; Heb. 5:7-9

THE LORD CREATING SUBMISSION

The Word of God tells us that the Lord Jesus and the Father are one. In the beginning was the Word, just as in the beginning there was God. The Word was God, and this Word created the heavens and earth. With God in the beginning there was glory. It was an inapproachable glory, the glory of the Son. The Father and the Son are equal, equipotent, coexisting, and existing simultaneously. But there is a difference in person between the Father and the Son. It is not a distinction in intrinsic nature but in arrangement in the Godhead. The Bible says that the Lord did not consider being equal with God a treasure to be grasped (Phil 2:6). To be grasped means to take by force. The Lord's equality with God is not something that He assumed by force. It is not an assertion or a usurpation because the Lord had the image of God in the first place.

Philippians 2:5-7 form one section, while verses 8-11 form another section. The first section is on Christ emptying Himself. The second section is on Christ humbling Himself. The Lord lowered Himself twice, first in emptying Himself in His deity, and then in humbling Himself in His humanity. When the Lord came down to earth, He emptied Himself of the glory, power, position, and image in His deity. As a result of His emptying, those without revelation did not recognize Him and would not acknowledge Him as God, considering Him merely as an ordinary man. In the Godhead the Lord voluntarily chose to be the Son, submitting Himself to the authority of the Father. Hence, He said that the Father was greater than He (John 14:28). The Son's position was a voluntary choice of our Lord. In the Godhead there is full harmony. In the Godhead there is equality, yet it is happily arranged that the Father should be the Head and that the Son should submit. The Father became the representation of authority, and the Son became the representation of submission.

We are human. Submission for us is simple. We can submit as long as we humble ourselves. But the Lord's submission is not a simple matter. The Lord's submission is more difficult than His creation of the heavens and the earth. In order to submit He had to empty Himself of all the glory, power, position, and image in His deity. He also had to take on the form of a slave. Only then could He receive the qualification of submission. Hence, submission is something created by the Son of God.

Formerly, the Father and the Son shared the same glory. When the Lord came down to earth, He dropped authority on the one hand and picked up submission on the other hand. He set His heart to become a slave, to be restricted in time and space as a man. But this is not all. The Lord humbled Himself, becoming obedient. The obedience in the Godhead is the most wonderful thing in the whole universe. He became obedient unto death, even the death of the cross, a painful and shameful death. In the end, God exalted Him to the highest. He that humbles himself will be exalted. This is God's principle.

THOSE FILLED WITH CHRIST
WILL BE FILLED WITH SUBMISSION

Originally, there was no need for submission in the Godhead. Because the Lord created submission, the Father became the Head to Christ in the Godhead. Both authority and submission were established by God. They were present from the beginning. Therefore, those who know the Lord will be submissive spontaneously. Those who do not know God nor Christ will not know authority or submission. With Christ there is the principle of submission. Those who accept submission are accepting the principle of Christ. Hence, those who are filled with Christ will be filled with submission.

Today many ask, "Why do I have to submit?" They also ask, "Why do I have to submit to you? I am a brother, and you are a brother." Actually, men do not have a right to say such things. Only the Lord is qualified to speak this way, but He never said such things. There was not even such a thought in Him. Christ represents submission, a perfect submission, just as God's authority is perfect authority. Today some think they know authority, but they do not know submission. We can only ask for God's mercy with such people.

THE WAY THE LORD CAME OUT
OF HIS DIVINE FORM
AND THE WAY HE RETURNED

Concerning His deity, the Lord was equal with God. But His being the Lord was something given to Him by God. Being made the Lord is something that happened after He emptied Himself in His deity. The deity of the Lord Jesus is something that is based on what He is. Being God is His original position. But His attainment of the position of Lord is based on what He has done. When He laid aside His divine form to fully maintain the principle of submission and subsequently ascended to the heavens, God accorded to Him the position of Lord. Based on Himself, He is God. Based on His attainment, He is Lord. This lordship was not originally present in the Godhead.

This portion in Philippians 2 is very difficult to explain and very controversial. But it is also a most divine passage. Today we have to come to this passage with our shoes off, standing on holy ground. It seems as if there was a conference in the Godhead in the beginning in which a plan was made to create the universe. In this plan the divine persons of the Godhead agreed with each other and came to the understanding that the Father would be the representation of authority. But if there was only authority without submission, authority could not be established, because authority is not something isolated. Hence, there must be submission in the universe. Two kinds of creatures were created in the universe. The first kind was the angels—spirits. The second kind was man—souls. God's foreknowledge foresaw the rebellion of the angels and the failure of man. God's authority cannot be built upon the angels or upon the descendants of Adam. In the Godhead there was a harmonious decision that authority would be established first within the Godhead. From that time on, there was a distinction in operation of the Father and the Son. One day the Son willingly emptied Himself to become a created man as the representation of submission to authority. It was the creature that had rebelled. Therefore, only the submission of a creature could establish God's authority. It was man who sinned and rebelled. Therefore, only through the submission of a man could God's authority be established. This is why the Lord had to come to the earth to become a man and to be the same as a creature in every way.

The birth of the Lord is the coming forth of God. He did not retain His authority by being God. Rather, He took up human restrictions by becoming a man, even the restriction of a slave. This was a very risky matter for the Lord. Once the Lord stepped out from the form of God, there was a possibility that He could not return as a man. If He had not been submissive, He could have reclaimed the divine form of His deity only in His position as the Son. However, the principle of submission would have been broken forever. When the Lord stepped out, there were only two ways for Him to return. One was to be a proper man, absolutely and unreservedly submitting with no trace of rebellion, being obedient step by step, and letting God bring Him back and set Him up as Lord. If being a slave had been too difficult for Him, if weakness and the limitations of the flesh had been too much for Him, and if submission had been beyond Him, the only other way to return would have been for Him to force His way back by using the authority and glory of His deity. But our Lord rejected this way, a way which He was not meant to take. He set His heart to subject Himself to the way of submission even unto death. Since He emptied Himself, He could no longer refill Himself. He did not vacillate in His mind. Since He emptied Himself of all divine glory and authority and stepped forth as a slave, He did not want to go back by any other way than the way of submission. Before He returned, He completed His course of being obedient unto death in the position of a man. He was able to return because He accomplished a perfect and pure submission. Suffering upon suffering was piled on Him, but He remained absolutely submissive. There was not the slightest reaction or rebellion. Therefore, God exalted Him and ushered Him back as Lord in the Godhead. This was not just a refilling of what had been emptied, but the ushering of a MAN into the Godhead by the Father. The Son became Jesus (the Man), and was received back into the Godhead. Now we know the preciousness of the name of Jesus. In the whole universe there is no one like Him. When the Lord declared, "It is done" on the cross, He did not mean that just salvation had been secured, but that everything that He said had been done. For this He obtained a name that is above every name. At the name of Jesus every knee should bow and every tongue should openly confess that Jesus Christ is Lord. From that time forward, He was not only God, but Lord as well. His lordship speaks of His relationship with God. It speaks of what He attained before God. His being the Christ speaks of His relationship with the church.

In short, when the Lord came forth from God, He did not intend to return by His deity. Rather, He intended to return through His exaltation as a man. This is how God maintains His principle of submission. It is wrong for us to have even a trace of rebellion. We should submit to authority completely. This is a great matter. The Lord Jesus' return to heaven was through His being a man and being submissive in the form of a man. As a result He was exalted by God. We must come face-to-face with this matter. In the whole Bible there is hardly any passage as mysterious as this one. The Lord bade farewell to His divine form. He did not return in just His divine form, because He had put on the flesh. In Him there was no trace of disobedience; consequently, He was exalted by God in His humanity. He stepped forth to give up His glory. He returned to reclaim His glory. All of this was accomplished by God. We need to have the mind in us which was in Christ Jesus. All of us should take the way of our Lord, taking His principle of submission as our principle unto submission and learning submission from one another. Whoever knows this principle will realize that no sin is uglier than rebellion and that nothing is more important than submission. Only when we see the principle of submission can we serve God. God's principle can be maintained only by submitting in the way that the Lord submitted. Once there is rebellion, we are in the principle of Satan.

LEARNING OBEDIENCE THROUGH SUFFERING

Hebrews 5:8 tells us that the Lord's obedience was learned through suffering. Suffering brought obedience to Him. True submission is found when there is still obedience in spite of suffering. A man's usefulness is not in whether he has suffered, but in whether he has learned obedience in suffering. Only those who are obedient to God are useful. If the heart is not softened, the suffering will not go away. Our way is the way of manifold sufferings. A man who yearns after ease and enjoyment is of no use. We must all learn to be obedient in sufferings. When the Lord came to the earth, He did not bring obedience with Him; rather, He learned it through sufferings.

Salvation not only brings joy; it also brings submission. If a man is only for joy, his experiences will not be abundant. Only submissive ones will experience the fullness of salvation. Otherwise, we change the nature of salvation. We need to be submissive, even as the Lord was submissive. The Lord became the source of our salvation through obedience. God saved us with the hope that we would submit to His will. When one meets God's authority, submission is a simple matter and knowing God's will is also a simple matter, because the Lord, who was submissive throughout His life, has already given us His life of submission.

CHAPTER SIX

HOW GOD ESTABLISHES HIS KINGDOM

Scripture Reading: Heb. 5:8-9; Acts 5:32; Rom. 10:16; 2 Thes. 1:8; 1 Pet. 1:22

THE LORD LEARNING OBEDIENCE THROUGH SUFFERING

God set up the principle of submission in the Lord. As a result, God established His authority through Him. In this chapter we want to see how God establishes His kingdom through submission. When the Lord came to the earth, He came empty-handed; He did not bring obedience with Him. He learned obedience through the sufferings He went through, and He became the cause of eternal salvation to all those who obey. His obedience on earth, even His death on the cross, was learned through times of suffering. Through all these sufferings He perfected His learning. The Lord came forth from the freedom of the Godhead to become a man, and He was made a weak and suffering man. Every suffering that the Lord went through bore fruits of obedience. All the sufferings of the Lord did not bring out any murmuring or complaint. However, many Christians pass through many years without learning obedience. Although their suffering increases, their obedience does not increase. When they experience sufferings, words of frustration often come from their mouths. This is a mark of not having learned obedience. The Lord went through all kind of sufferings. His submission was manifested in everything. As a consequence, His submission became the cause of our salvation. Through the obedience of One many received grace. The Lord's obedience is for the kingdom of God. The goal of redemption is the increase of the kingdom of God.

GOD DESIRES TO ESTABLISH HIS KINGDOM

Have you ever realized how much the universe was affected by the fall of the angels and man and how big a problem this made for God? God desired that His creatures would accept His authority; however, both kinds of creatures rejected His authority. God was unable to establish His authority over the creatures. Nevertheless, God did not call back His authority. God can call back His presence, but He will never call back His system of authority. Wherever God's authority is, God is given a position of prominence. On the one hand, God maintains His system of authority, and on the other hand, He establishes His kingdom. Although Satan rebelled against God's authority, and although man daily violates His authority by rebelling against Him, God will not let this rebellion continue. He will establish His own kingdom. The Bible calls the kingdom of God the kingdom of the heavens because rebellion is not limited to just the world (Matt. 4:17; Mark 1:15). The angels in the heavens rebelled as well.

How did the Lord establish God's kingdom? He did it through submission. Whatever the Lord did on earth was entirely based on submission. He did nothing that opposed God's authority. Everything was in submission, in perfect cooperation with the authority of God. In this realm the Lord set up the kingdom of God and executed His authority. The church today must also allow God's authority to have a free way and manifest His kingdom through submission.

GOD DESIRES THAT THE CHURCH
BE THE KINGDOM OF GOD

After Adam fell, God chose Noah and his family in his generation. After the flood this family also fell, and God chose Abraham to be the father of many nations. The kingdom of God was built upon him. Then He chose Isaac and Jacob. Later, the descendants of Jacob suffered in Egypt. In their sufferings, their number multiplied. God then sent Moses to lead them out of Egypt in order to establish a kingdom. Because of the rebellious ones among them, God led them through the wilderness to teach them obedience before He would establish the kingdom (Deut. 8:3). But they were still rebellious against God in the wilderness. As a result, all were strewn along in the wilderness. Even though the second generation entered, they were not yet fully obedient; they did not completely drive out the Canaanites. Saul, their first king, was not able to establish the kingdom because of rebellion. We do not find the first king after God's heart until David was chosen and became submissive to God's authority. But there was still rebellion within the kingdom. It was God's command that Jerusalem be the place where His name should be set, but the people chose Gibeon and set up altars there. Because of the lack of submission, there was no content to the kingdom even though there was a king. Before David there was a kingdom without the people. During David's time there was a people with the kingdom, but without the content of a kingdom. For that reason, the kingdom of God was still not established.

The Lord came to the earth to establish God's kingdom. There are two sides to the gospel. On the one hand, there is the individual aspect. On the other hand, there is the corporate aspect. Individually, the gospel gives eternal life to those who believe. Corporately, the gospel calls people to repentance unto the kingdom of God. God's eyes are upon the kingdom. In the Lord's prayer in Matthew 6:9-13, the kingdom is spoken of at the beginning and the end. Verse 10 says, "Your kingdom come; Your will be done, as in heaven, so also on earth." The kingdom of God is the sphere where His will is accomplished in an unhindered way. Verse 13 says, "For Yours is the kingdom and the power and the glory forever. Amen." The kingdom, the power, and glory are related. Revelation 12:10 says, "Now has come the salvation and the power and the kingdom of our God and the authority of His Christ." The kingdom is the sphere of authority. In Luke 17:21 the Lord said, "For behold, the kingdom of God is in the midst of you." (He did not say that it is in you.) This word indicates that the Lord Jesus is the kingdom of God. For the Lord Jesus to be in the midst of you is for the kingdom of God to be in the midst of you, because the authority of God is fully executed in Him. The kingdom of God is upon the Lord. It is also upon the church. Because the Lord's life has been released to the church, His kingdom must also be propagated and established through the church. From the time of Noah, God established a kingdom. But that was just a kingdom of man; it was not the kingdom of God. The kingdom of God began with the Lord Jesus, but how small was its sphere! Today the one grain of wheat has produced many grains. Today the sphere of the kingdom of God is not limited to the Lord alone. It is also in the many believers.

God's purpose is not only for us to become the church, but also for the church to become the kingdom of God. She is to be the sphere of God's kingdom, the place where God executes His authority. Hence, God's desire is not only to gain ground in a few, but to have the whole church free from rebellion. There must be an absolute submission and an absolute position for God so that His authority can be perfectly carried out. In this way authority is established among God's creatures. Not only does God want man to submit to His direct authority, He wants man to submit to all of His appointed, deputy authorities as well. God does not ask for a little submission; He demands a perfect submission.

THE GOSPEL BEING NOT ONLY
FOR MAN TO BELIEVE BUT ALSO FOR MAN TO SUBMIT

The Bible speaks not only of faith. It also speaks of obedience. We are not only sinners; we are sons of disobedience. In Romans 10:16 we have the obedience to the gospel. In principle believing in the gospel is obeying the gospel. Second Thessalonians 1:8 says, "Rendering vengeance to those who do not know God and to those who do not obey the gospel of our Lord Jesus Christ." Those who do not obey are those who rebel. Romans 2:8 speaks of those who are disobedient to the truth. This is also rebellion, and God will render wrath and anger to those who rebel against the truth. First Peter 1:22 says, "Since you have purified your souls by your obedience to the truth..." By this we see that salvation comes through obedience. To believe is to obey. A disciple in faith should really be a disciple in obedience. Not only must there be the faith; there must also be the submission to the Lord's authority. When Paul was enlightened, he said, "What shall

I do, Lord?" (Acts 22:10). He not only believed in the Lord; he became obedient to the Lord. Paul's conversion not only made him realize grace, but also made him submit to authority. When he was moved by the Holy Spirit to see the authority of the gospel, he acknowledged Jesus as Lord.

God has called us not only to receive life through faith, but also to maintain His authority through obedience. God's plan for us in the church is for us to submit to His authority and to all the authorities He has established. This covers our home, our government, our school, the church, and so forth. He does not want to specifically mark out whom we should submit to. As long as we have met God's authority in the Lord, we should learn to submit to authority.

Many can submit and be obedient if they are under certain ones, but to others they cannot submit. This is due to a failure in seeing authority. It is useless to submit to man. What is needed is to see authority. All kinds of systems are for us to learn submission. After a man has touched authority, a slight disobedience will cause him to have an inward sense of rebellion. Those who do not know authority do not realize how rebellious they are. Before Paul was enlightened, he did not know that he was kicking against the goads (26:14). After a man is enlightened, he will first see authority. Then he will see many authorities. When Paul met a little brother, Ananias, he did not see just a man. He did not ask who Ananias was or whether or not he was educated. He recognized Ananias as a sent authority, a deputy authority. Therefore, Paul submitted to him (9:17-18). How easy it is to submit when one has met authority!

GOD DESIRES TO MAKE THE NATIONS
THE KINGDOM OF GOD THROUGH THE CHURCH

If the church does not take God's authority, He has no way to establish His kingdom. First, God gained the kingdom in the Lord Jesus. Then He established His kingdom in the church. In the end His kingdom will be established on the whole earth. One day there will be a declaration, "The kingdom of the world has become the kingdom of our Lord and of His Christ" (Rev. 11:15). Between the time in which the kingdom was in the Lord Jesus individually and the kingdom of the world becomes the kingdom of our Lord and of His Christ, there is the church. Only when the kingdom was established in the Lord Jesus could it be established in the church. Only when the kingdom is established in the church can the kingdom of the world become the kingdom of God. Without the Lord Jesus, there is no church. Without the church, there is no expansion of the kingdom of God.

When the Lord was on earth, He was obedient even in the smallest thing. For example, He was not negligent in the matter of paying the temple tax. Even when there was no money, a coin was found in the mouth of a fish to pay it (Matt. 17:24-27). He also said, "Render then the things that are Caesar's to Caesar and the things that are God's to God" (22:21). Although Caesar was rebellious, he was set up by God, and as such, one must obey him. When our obedience is perfect, the Lord will rebuke the disobedient ones. When we become submissive, the kingdom can be expanded to the whole earth. Many have strong feelings concerning sin, but they have no feeling concerning rebellion. Man must not only have the consciousness of sin; he must also have the consciousness of authority. Without the consciousness of sin, one cannot be a disciple of Christ. Without the consciousness of authority, one cannot be a disciple of submission.

THE CHURCH MUST SUBMIT TO GOD'S AUTHORITY

We have to know how to submit in the church. There is not a single authority in the church that we can ignore. God wants to see the kingdom issuing forth from the church. He wants all authority to be executed through the church. When the church is so submissive, the earth will submit to the authority of God. If the church will not give the kingdom of God a free way, the kingdom of God will have no way among the nations. For this reason, the church is the highway to the kingdom. If this is not the case, the church will become a hindrance to the kingdom.

Today if the church cannot submit to God because of a little difficulty, how can the kingdom of God be manifested? When men reason with one another and argue with one another, how can God's kingdom come? We have delayed God. We must rid ourselves of all disobedience so that God will have a free way. When the church submits, the nations will submit. For this reason, the church bears a great and heavy responsibility. When God's life, God's will, and God's commands are executed in the church, the kingdom will come.

CHAPTER SEVEN

GOD INTENDS THAT MAN SUBMIT TO REPRESENTATIVE AUTHORITY

Scripture Reading: Rom. 13:1; 1 Pet. 2:13-14; Eph. 5:22-24; 6:1-3; Col. 3:18, 20, 22; 1 Thes. 5:12-13; 1 Tim. 5:17; 1 Pet. 5:5; 1 Cor. 16:15-16

THE GOD-ESTABLISHED SYSTEMS OF AUTHORITY

In the World

In the universe God is the source of all authorities. All authorities on earth are set up by Him. As such, they represent God's authority and even possess God's authority. God Himself has set up systems of authorities for His expression so that when man meets these authorities he will meet God Himself. When the presence of God is available, man can know God through His presence. When the presence of God is absent, man can meet God by meeting His authority. In the garden of Eden when God's presence was there, man could know God. When God was not present, man could remind himself of God's commandment, which was the prohibition concerning the eating of the fruit. This was another way for man to know God. It is not often that man meets God in the world. (This, of course, does not include the fact that in the church, when man lives in the spirit, he can contact God all the time.) God's manifestation is seen most frequently in His commandments. Only the foolish vinedressers need the personal appearance of the owner of the vineyard. In reality, the servants and the owner's son were enough to represent him (Mark 12:1-9).

Some are set up by God to give commands and to be authorities for God. All those in authority are ordained by God. Hence, all authorities that God has set up should be honored. Today God has entrusted authority to man. After entrusting man with authority, many on earth have been set up by God to manifest His authority. If we want to learn submission to God, we should know to whom the authority of God is entrusted. If we understand God's authority as being only in Himself, it is very likely that we will offend God's authority more than half of the time. How many people are there in whom we see God's authority? There is no such thing as making a choice between God's direct authority and His deputy authority. Not only do we have to submit to God's direct authority, we must also submit to His deputy authority because there is no authority that is not from God.

Concerning earthly authority, Paul gave not only a positive word about submission, but also a negative warning that resisting authority is the same as resisting God's personal commandment (Rom. 13:1). For man to reject God's deputy authority is for him to reject God's own authority. In the Bible authority bears only one nature. There is no authority that is not of God. To resist authority is to resist God. God will not overlook this. Those who oppose will receive to themselves judgment. It is impossible for us to rebel without being punished. Hence, for man to resist authority is to incur death. In the matter of authority there is no choice.

At the time of Adam, God committed governmental authority to man and charged him to rule the earth (Gen. 1:28). At that time man ruled only the animals. It was not until the time of the flood that God entrusted to Noah the governmental authority to rule over man. He said, "Whoso sheddeth man's blood, by man shall his blood be shed" (9:6). From that time on, God committed to man the authority to rule over man. From the time of Noah, God began to set up governments, and He put man under governments.

In Exodus 20, after God's people left Egypt and had come to the wilderness, the Ten Commandments were given. Following that, there were the ordinances concerning the people's conduct. Among these ordinances, one says, "Thou shalt not...curse the ruler of thy people" (22:28). This proves that God had placed them under governmental authorities. Therefore, even in the time of Moses, we can already see that the Israelites' resistance to authority was their resistance to God.

All of the nations on the earth have rulers. Although they do not believe in God, and although their entire kingdoms are under Satan, the principle of authority is still there, having been established by God. The kingdom of Israel was God's kingdom. King David, of course, was set up by God. But the king of Persia was also set up by God (Isa. 45:1). When the Lord was on the earth, He likewise submitted to the government and to the authority of the high priest. This is why the Lord paid the tax and why He said that what belongs to Caesar should be rendered to Caesar. When He was judged by the high priest, who adjured Him by God, He had to obey. The Lord recognized them as earthly authorities. He never tried to stir up a revolution.

In Romans 13:4 Paul showed us that all rulers are the servants of God. At that time the government was in the hand of the Romans. Humanly speaking, there is no need to submit to foreign aggressors. But Paul did not tell us to rebel against a foreign government. Not only do we have to submit to our own nation and to our own race, we have to submit to the government wherever we are as well. I cannot disobey a local government just because I am of another nationality. The law is not a terror to the good, but to the evil. No matter how different the laws of the various nations are, they are all from the law of God. Their basic principle is still the rewarding of good and the punishing of evil. Every government has its laws, and the function of the government is to maintain and execute the laws so that the good would be rewarded and the evil would be punished. They do not bear the sword in vain. Although there are governments that uphold evil and suppress good, they must of necessity change the truth, calling the evil good and the good evil. At any rate, they cannot say that they are upholding such and such because they are evil or that they are punishing such and such because they are good. To this day all governments uphold the principle of the reward of good and the punishment of evil. This principle is irrevocable. For this reason we say that the governments still adhere to God's principle. One day when the lawless one (the Antichrist) appears, he will overturn all authorities. That will be the end of the world. By then the good will, indeed, be taken as evil and the evil as good. The good will be killed and the evil will rule.

There are four signs of submission to authority on earth: rendering (1) tax to whom tax is due, (2) custom to whom custom is due, (3) fear to whom fear is due, and (4) honor to whom honor is due.

For a Christian, abiding by the law is not something done out of fear of punishment but out of the exercise of his conscience before God. If he does not submit, his conscience will be condemned. This is why we have to learn to submit to our local government. God's children cannot criticize or revile the government lightly. Even the policeman on the street is a God-established authority. He is God's officer attending constantly to this very thing. What should our attitude be when it comes to paying taxes and revenue? Do we consider our local government as God's authority? Are we submissive to it? If man has not met authority, he cannot submit. The more you ask such a one to submit, the harder it is for him to do so. Second Peter 2:10 refers to "those who go after the flesh in the lust for defilement and despise lordship. Daring, self-willed, they do not tremble while reviling dignities." There are many whose power has been lost and whose life has drained away through reviling. Man must not fall into anarchy. The way that God deals with an unrighteous government is not our concern. Of course, when we pray for God to execute His righteousness, it is a different matter. But for us, any disobedience to authority is disobedience to God's authority. If we are not submissive, we are actually strengthening the principle of the Antichrist. When the mystery of lawlessness operates, are we its restraints or are we its helpers?

In the Family

God has established His authority in the family. Many children of God do not pay enough attention to the matter of the family. But in the Epistles, especially in Ephesians and Colossians, the two books with the highest spirituality, the matter of the family is not overlooked. In particular, they speak of submission in the family. Neglect of this matter will cause trouble in God's service. First Timothy and Titus are books on work, but they also speak of the family, lest the family affect the work. First Peter is a book particularly on the kingdom, and in this book we see that to rebel against authority in the family is to rebel against the kingdom. When man meets authority, family problems decrease.

God establishes the husband as the deputy authority of Christ, and the wife as the representation of the church. Unless the wife sees the authority that the husband represents, the authority that God has set up, it is difficult for her to submit. She has to see that it is not a matter of her husband but a matter of God's authority. Titus 2:5 says young women should be "subject to their own husbands, that the word of God would not be blasphemed." First Peter 3:1 says, "In like manner, wives, be subject to your own husbands, that even if any disobey the word, they will be gained without the word through the manner of life of their wives." Verses 5 and 6 say, "For in this manner formerly the holy women also, who hoped in God, adorned themselves, being subject to their own husbands, as Sarah obeyed Abraham, calling him lord."

Ephesians 6:1-3 says, "Children, obey your parents in the Lord, for this is right. 'Honor your father and mother,' which is the first commandment with a promise, 'That it may be well with you and that you may live long on the earth.'" Of the Ten Commandments, this one has special reward. When a man honors his parents, he will be blessed and live long on the earth. Many probably die early because they do not honor their parents. Some brothers are at odds with their parents. Hence, they are often sick. Not until they become obedient will they become well. Colossians 3:20 says, "Children, obey your parents in all things, for this is well pleasing in the Lord." We have to submit ourselves to our parents' authority. This also requires that we first see God's authority.

Servants should obey their masters, even as they obey the Lord. In their attitude they should be in fear and trembling, not being deceitful or crafty, rendering only eye-service. Whether one sees his master or not, he has to serve just the same. He should not serve only within the sphere of his master's sight, but should rather serve according to the honesty in the heart, not as unto man, but as unto the Lord, for we serve the Lord Christ. First Timothy 6:1 says, "As many as are slaves under the yoke should regard their own masters as worthy of all honor, lest the name of God and our teaching be blasphemed." Titus 2:9-10 says, "Exhort slaves to be subject to their own masters in all things, to be well pleasing, not contradicting, not pilfering, but showing all good faithfulness that they may adorn the teaching of our Savior God in all things." You must first uphold the Lord's authority yourself, and then others will uphold the Lord's authority which is with you. When Paul and Peter said these words, they were still under the Roman Empire where slave trading was very prevalent. Whether or not the system of slavery is right is one thing, but God ordains that slaves should obey their masters.

In the Church

God has His appointed authorities in the church. They are the elders who take the lead well and those who labor in word and teaching. God commands that all should submit to them. In addition, all the younger ones should submit to the older ones. First Peter 5:5 says, "In like manner, younger men, be subject to elders." Chapter five speaks of those who are elderly in age, while 1 Corinthians 16:15 speaks of the household of Stephanas as "the firstfruits of Achaia (indicating seniority in the order of salvation), and they have set themselves to minister to the saints." Stephanas was exceedingly humble and had set himself to minister to the saints. In verse 16 the apostle further said, "You also be subject to such ones, and to everyone co-working and laboring."

In the church the woman also has to submit to the man. First Corinthians 11:3 says, "But I want you to know that Christ is the head of every man, and the man is the head of the woman, and God is the head of Christ." God appointed man to be the authority as a type of Christ and the woman to submit as a type of the church. For this reason the woman should have authority on her head for the sake of the angels.

Furthermore, the woman must submit to her husband. First Corinthians 14:34 says, "The women should be silent in the churches, for they are not permitted to speak; but they should be subject, even as the law also says." If there is anything that they want to learn, they can ask their husbands at home. Some sisters may ask, "What if my husband does not know?" If God tells you to ask, just go and ask. If you keep asking, your husband will know after a period of time. Because he is being asked, he will have to seek to understand in order to answer. In this way you help yourself and you help your husband as well. First Timothy 2:11 also speaks of women learning in "quietness in all subjection." Women are not permitted to exercise authority over a man, for Adam was formed first, then Eve (vv. 12-13).

Among God's children, everyone should gird himself with humility and should submit one to another. Some like to pretentiously show off their position or authority. This is low and shameful.

Not only has God set up His deputy authority in the universe, He has also set up His authority in the spiritual world. Second Peter 2:10-11 says, "Especially those who go after the flesh in the lust for defilement and despise lordship. Daring, self-willed, they do not tremble while reviling dignities; whereas angels, though they are greater in strength and power, do not bring a reviling judgment against them before the Lord." Here we have a very important matter. In the spiritual universe there are lordships and dignities, and God has put even angels under them. Although some lords and dignities failed, the angels still dare not revile them today, for these lords and dignities were once their authorities. Today, even though some lords and dignities have fallen, the other angels can only mention the facts. They cannot pass on their judgments. If they add their judgments to the facts, they are reviling. Jude 9 says, "Michael the archangel, when he contended with the devil and disputed concerning the body of Moses, did not dare to bring a reviling judgment against him but said, The Lord rebuke you." At one time God set up Satan to be the head of the archangels. As one of the archangels, Michael was under Satan's authority at one time.

One day Moses will resurrect. Perhaps it will be on the mount of transfiguration. Michael followed God's command to look for the body of Moses, but Satan deterred him. Michael could have countered the rebellious spirit with a rebellious spirit. He could have rebuked Satan in a flagrant way, but Michael dared not do this. He only said, "The Lord rebuke you." (It is different with human beings. God never put human beings under Satan. We have fallen under his power; we were never put under his authority.) The same principle applies to David. Once he was under Saul, the deputy authority of God; therefore, he dared not overturn Saul's former authority. How dignified is a deputy authority in spiritual matters! It cannot be reviled. The ones who revile will lose their spiritual power.

Once you touch authority, you will see God's authority wherever you go. The first question you should ask is to whom you should submit and to whose word you should listen. A Christian should have two kinds of feelings: one is the feeling of sin, and the other is the feeling of authority. When two brothers are together discussing or considering ideas, both can speak. But when the time of decision comes, one makes the judgment. Acts 15 records a big conference. Everyone, whether old or young, was free to rise up to speak. Every brother could speak. Later Peter and Paul spoke. Then James made the decision. Peter and Paul gave the facts; James made the decision. There was a lining up even among the elders and apostles. Paul said that he was the least among the apostles (1 Cor. 15:9). There is even a distinction between great and small among the apostles. This is not a matter of someone lining us up. Rather, it involves knowing our proper position. This is the most beautiful testimony and the most wonderful picture. This makes Satan tremble, and this will bring down his kingdom. When we all take the way of submission, God will judge the world.

WE SHOULD HAVE CONFIDENCE
IN SUBMITTING TO THE DELEGATED AUTHORITY

What a dangerous risk it is for God to set up authorities for Himself! How much He suffers if the delegated authorities He has set up wrongly represent Him! But God is confident in the authority that He establishes. It is much easier for us to be confident in submitting to representative authorities than for God to be confident in setting them up. Since God is confident in handing over authority to man, should we not be confident in submitting to man? We should be confident in submitting to the authority which God is confident in establishing. If there is a mistake, it is not our mistake. It is the mistake of the authority. The Lord says that every person should be subject to the authorities over him (Rom. 13:1). There is more difficulty on God's part than on our part. When God trusts man, we can as well. When God is confident about His trust, we should be even more so.

Luke 9:48 says, "Whoever receives this little child because of My name receives Me; and whoever receives Me receives Him who sent Me." There is no problem for the Lord to represent the Father, because the Father has entrusted everything to Him. For us to believe in Him is to believe in the Father. But in the Lord's eyes even a child can represent the Lord. The Lord can entrust Himself to a child. This is why He said that receiving a little child is to receive the Lord. In Luke 10:16 the Lord sent out the disciples and said, "He who hears you hears Me, and he who rejects you rejects Me." All of the disciples' words, charges, decisions, and opinions represented the Lord. The Lord was so confident that He entrusted all authority to the disciples. Whatever they said in the Lord's name, He acknowledged. Therefore, rejecting the disciples was the same as rejecting the Lord. The Lord could entrust Himself to them with full peace. He did not say that they should be careful in their words or that they should not blunder in speaking when they went out. The Lord was not concerned at all with what would happen if they blundered. The Lord had the faith and the courage to hand over authority to the disciples with confidence.

But the Jews were not like this. They doubted and said, "How can this be? How do I know that all you said is right? We need more considerations!" They dared not believe. They were very afraid. Suppose you are working as an executive in a corporation, and you send one out saying, "Do your best. Whatever you do I will acknowledge. When people listen to you, they are listening to me." If this is the case, you would probably require him to send back a daily report of his work, lest there be any mistake. But the Lord can entrust us to be His representatives. What a big trust this is! Since the Lord trusts His deputy authority so much, we should trust such authority even more.

Some may say, "What happens if the authority makes mistakes?" If God dares to trust those who are entrusted as authorities, then we should dare to submit. Whether or not the authority makes mistakes has nothing to do with us. In other words, whether the deputy authority is right or wrong is a matter for which he has to be responsible directly before the Lord. Those who submit to authority need only to submit absolutely. Even if they make a mistake through submission, the Lord will not reckon that as sin. The Lord will hold the deputy authority responsible for that sin. To disobey is to rebel. For this the submitting one has to be responsible before God. For this reason there is no human element involved in submission. If we are only submitting to a person, the meaning of authority is lost. Moreover, since God has already set up His deputy authority, He must maintain this authority. Whether or not others are right is their business. Whether or not I am right is my business. Everyone has to be responsible to the Lord for himself.

REJECTING DEPUTY AUTHORITY BEING
TO REJECT GOD HIMSELF

The whole parable in Luke 20:9-16 is on deputy authority. God leased the vineyard to the vinedresser, but He did not come to personally collect the rent. The first, second, and third time He sent His servants; the fourth time He sent His Son. All of these were His representatives. God could have come Himself, but instead He sent His representative. In God's eyes all those who rejected His servants rejected Him. We cannot hearken to God's word, yet refuse the word of His deputy authority. We have to submit to God's authority as well as to His deputy authority. Other than in Acts 9:4-15, which speaks of the Lord's direct authority, the Lord entrusts His authority to deputy authorities in both the Old Testament and the New Testament. One may say that almost all authorities are entrusted to man. Many think that this means submitting to man. But if you have met authority, you will know that this is God's deputy authority. There is no need for humility for one to submit to God's direct authority. But there must be humility and brokenness for one to submit to the deputy authority. Only by laying the flesh completely aside can one accept and obey the deputy authority. We constantly have to see that God does not come personally to collect His rent. God sends representatives to collect rent. What should we do with God? Should we wait for God to come personally? When He comes personally, it will not be for rent, but for judgment.

The Lord showed Paul at one point that for him to withstand the Lord was to kick against the goads (Acts 26:14). When Paul saw the light, he saw authority as well. He said, "What shall I do, Lord?" (22:10). This was Paul putting himself directly under the Lord's own authority. But then the Lord placed Paul under His appointed deputy authority. The Lord said, "Rise up and enter into the city, and it will be told to you what you must do" (9:6). From that time on Paul knew authority. He did not say, "It is so rare that I meet the Lord Himself; let Him tell me what to do." At that time, the Lord placed Paul under a deputy authority. It did not please the Lord to tell Paul directly. From the time we have believed in the Lord until now, how many deputy authorities have we submitted to? How many times have we submitted to them? Prior to this, we did not have the light, but today we have to see in a serious way God's deputy authority. We have been talking about submission for five or ten years, but how much have we submitted to indirect authorities? What God looks at is not His own direct authority. He looks at His established, indirect authorities. All those who do not submit to God's indirect authorities cannot submit to God's direct authority.

For the sake of clarity in explanation, we have differentiated between direct authority and indirect authority. Actually, in God's eyes it is just one authority. We cannot despise authority in the family or in the church. We cannot despise any deputy authority. Although Paul was blind, it was as if he were waiting for Ananias with open eyes. When he saw Ananias, it was as if he saw the Lord. When he listened to Ananias, it was as if he was listening to the Lord. The deputy authority involves such serious matters that if you offend him you get into trouble with God. It is impossible for you to reject light from the deputy authority and hope to receive light from the Lord. Paul did not say, "Since Cornelius asked for Peter, I also can ask God to send Peter or James. I do not want this little brother Ananias to be my authority." It is impossible for us to reject the deputy authority and to submit to God directly. This is because the rejection of deputy authority is a rejection of the Lord Himself. Only foolish ones will want the deputy authority to fail. He who dislikes God's representative dislikes God Himself. Man's rebellious nature likes to submit to God's direct authority, but reject God's appointed deputy authority.

GOD HONORING HIS DEPUTY AUTHORITY

Numbers 30 speaks of a woman's vow. When a woman was young in her father's house, her father had to silently acknowledge the vow before it would become effective. If the father disallowed it, the vow would not stand. If she was married, then the vow had to be silently acknowledged by the husband. If the husband disallowed it, then the vow was annulled (vv. 3-8). When the deputy authority consents, the direct authority fulfills it. If the deputy authority disallows it, the direct authority disowns it. God is pleased with having deputy authority. He also honors the deputy authority. When a woman is under the authority of her husband, God will not uphold her vow as long as the husband disallows it. God only wants her to submit to authority. But if the deputy authority is wrong, God will deal with him; he will have to bear the iniquity of his wife, and the submitting wife is guiltless (v. 15). This chapter tells us that man cannot overstep the deputy authority to submit to the direct authority. Since God has handed out His authority, even He Himself will not overstep His deputy authority. Even He Himself is bound by the deputy authority. God establishes through the establishment of the deputy authority, and He annuls through the annulling of the deputy authority. God wants to maintain His deputy authority. Therefore, we have only one way with the deputy authority, which is the way of submission.

The whole New Testament upholds deputy authority. Only in Acts 5:29, when the Sanhedrin persecuted Peter by forbidding him to preach in the Lord's name, did Peter say, "It is necessary to obey God rather than men." Only when the deputy authority obviously defies God's commandment and offends the Lord's person can we refuse the deputy authority. Hence, this kind of word can only be spoken under such a circumstance. Other than this, we have to submit to the deputy authority in any other circumstance. We cannot be careless. We must not fulfill submission by exercising rebellion.

CHAPTER EIGHT

AUTHORITY IN THE BODY

Scripture Reading: 1 Cor. 12:12-21; Matt. 18:15-18

THE BODY BEING THE PLACE
FOR THE HIGHEST EXPRESSION OF AUTHORITY

The highest expression of God's authority is in the Body of Christ, the church. Although God has established systems of authority in the world, none of the relationships with the government or between father and son, husband and wife, and master and servant can perfectly manifest authority. Although God has set up many authorities on earth, they are but systems of authority set up by God. Man can obey them outwardly without submitting to them inwardly. For example, if the government passes an edict, the people can obey it from their heart, or they can obey it, but not from the heart. There is no way to tell which kind of obedience is present. Likewise, there is no way to tell whether a child's submission to his parents is from the heart or if it is merely superficial or behavioral. Hence, submission to authority cannot be typified by a child's submission to his parents or a servant's submission to his master, much less a people's submission to its government. Without submission there is, of course, no establishment of God's authority. An outward submission that has no inward correspondence still does not establish God's authority. Moreover, many kinds of submission are based upon man's relationship with man—for example, a father with a son or a master with a servant. But master and servant can be separated, and so can father and son. Hence, we do not see absolute and perfect submission in these relationships.

Only Christ and the church have the highest expression

of authority and submission. God has not established the church to make it an organization, but to make it the Body of Christ. We think that the church is the gathering together of believers of the same faith, or that it is a gathering together in love. But God sees it differently. The church is not only a convergence in faith or love; it is a body. The church is the Body of Christ, and Christ is the Head of the church. Father and son, master and servant, or even husband and wife can be separated, but the body and the head can never be separated. They are forever joined as one. In the same way Christ and the church can never be separated one from the other. With Christ and the church there is an absolute submission and an absolute authority which are far above all other authorities and submissions. Although the parents love their children, they may make mistakes. They may misuse their authority. Likewise, a government can also give wrong orders, and a master's authority can also be wrong. Not only is submission imperfect in the world, but authority is also imperfect. For this reason God has to establish a perfect authority and a perfect submission, which is Christ and the church, the Head and the Body. There are some parents who would harm their children; there are husbands who would harm their wives; there are masters who would harm their servants; and there are rulers who would harm their subjects. But there is no head that would harm its own body. Hence, the authority of the head cannot be wrong; it is perfect. Look at the submission of the body to the head; it is also perfect. As long as the head has any desire, the finger will move. There is no need for words; there is no need of force. Everything is so harmonious. God's will is that we submit perfectly. We must be brought by God to a condition that is like the body submitting to the head. Only then will God be satisfied. This cannot be represented by the husband and the wife and so forth. Authority is of Him, and submission is likewise of Him. Authority and submission are one thing. It is not like the world, where authority and submission are two different things. For a body to move, there is no need for the head to exert strength to give command. As soon as a thought arises, the body will move. There is perfect harmony in this. If we can only submit to the degree that the children are submissive to parents or wives are submissive to husbands, God will not be satisfied. God desires that our submission be like that of the body submitting to the head. It is not a submission by coercion, such as that which is seen in the nations. Rather, it is a submission of the body to the head. As soon as the head has a little intention, there is a harmonious submission.

If you have submitted yourself to God often, you realize that God's command and God's will are entirely different. His command is a word out of His mouth, and His will is an idea out of His heart. A command must be uttered, but a will need not be uttered. The Lord Jesus was submissive not only to God's word but also to His will. Whenever there was a will, the Lord moved and acted. God must wrought into Christ and the church a relationship like that between Christ and the Father. God must work in us until we can submit to Christ in the same way that Christ submits to God. In the first part of His work, God made Himself the Head of Christ. In the second part of His work, He made Christ the Head of the church. He has to work until there is submission even without the need of the dealing of the Holy Spirit. As soon as He has a desire, we will immediately obey. In the third part of God's work, God will make the kingdoms of the earth the kingdom of the Lord and of His Christ. The first part has already been accomplished, and the third part is yet to come. Today we are in the middle part. If the work in the second part is not complete, the third part cannot commence. Are we here to submit and give God a free way, or are we here to disobey and hinder God? God has never secured authority in the universe. The place where His authority will see a complete success and the place where the tide is turned is the church. The church is the middle part; it is the turning point. For this reason God reserves the greatest glory for us. Without seeing authority there is no way to go on. If this matter is not resolved in us, it will not be resolved in others. We all bear the responsibility of expressing authority.

IT BEING MOST SPONTANEOUS AND HARMONIOUS
FOR THE BODY TO SUBMIT TO THE HEAD

Today God has made everything ready. The Body and the Head already have the same life and nature. Therefore, submission is very spontaneous, while not being submissive is rather strange. For example, if the hand is raised up according to the desire of the head, there is nothing strange about it. But if the hand cannot move, then it is a strange thing. Perhaps the hand is sick. The Spirit of life that God gave to us is the same as that which is in the Lord. The life and the nature that He gave us is likewise the same as that in the Lord. Here again there is no possibility of disharmony and disobedience. Some of our bodily movements are conscious, while others are unconscious. The oneness of the body with the head does not depend only on a conscious submission, but on an unconscious submission. It is like breathing. There can be conscious deep breathing or there can be unconscious and spontaneous ordinary breathing. This is like the heart which beats without consciousness. There is no need to give it an order; it keeps on beating by itself. This is submission in life. For the body to submit to the head, there is no noise, no imposition, and no friction. Everything is in harmony. It is not enough for some to just submit to commands. In the commands is the will, and in the will is the law of life. Only when one submits to the law of life is his submission perfect. If the submission is not like that of the body submitting to the head, it is not called submission. The submission of some is with such reluctance that it cannot be considered as submission.

The Lord has put us into the Body. Here the union is perfect and the submission is perfect. It is a wonder that even the mind of the Holy Spirit can be guided by the members. There is no possibility of separating two members from the other to make them distinct wholes. A harmony spontaneously exists between the members. There is no need to even think about this submission. Its harmony is beyond the description of human words, and its submission to authority is the most perfect that can be found. For this reason we cannot be a sick member, one that makes noise and causes friction. We are living in the operation of God's authority; there should be a very spontaneous submission. The church is not only the place of fellowship for the brothers and sisters; it is also the place for the manifestation of authority.

REJECTING THE AUTHORITY IN THE MEMBERS BEING TO REJECT THE HEAD

The authority in the Body is sometimes not manifested directly, but indirectly. Not only does the body submit to the head; its members submit to and help one another also. The left and the right hands do not have direct fellowship with each other. The head moves the right hand, and the head moves the left hand. The left hand does not control the right hand, nor the right hand the left. The hand does not order the eyes to see. It only informs the head. The head then directs the eyes to see. No matter how far the members are from the head, their relationship with the head is the same, and all their works relate back to the head. If my eyes see, my hands work, or my feet move, then I say that I see, I work, or I move. Hence, many times the decision of the members is the decision of the head. The authority of the members is the authority of the head. The hand cannot see by itself; it needs the decision of the eyes. It is wrong for the hand either to ask the head to see or to ask itself to see. Both are impossible. But this is often the problem with God's children. Hence, we must take other members as the deputy authority of the Head. The function of the hand is just that of a hand, the function of the foot is only that of a foot, and the function of the eyes is only that of the eyes. We must accept others' function as our function. We cannot reject the function of the members. If the foot rejects the hand, it is rejecting the head. Consequently, when we accept the authority of the members, we are accepting the authority of the Head. Every member is my authority in fellowship. Although the function of the hand is great, it has to accept the function of the foot in the matter of walking. The hand cannot feel color; it needs the authority of the eyes. The function of the members is the authority of the members.

AUTHORITY BEING THE RICHES OF CHRIST

Today it is impossible for every member to be the whole Body. For this reason everyone should stand in his position as a member, receiving the function of the other members. When others see and hear, then I see and hear. Receiving the function of the members is receiving the riches of the Head. There is no one member who is independent. I am only a member. A member cannot do the work of the Body. What the other members have done is what the Body has done. It is also what each member has done. In today's situation, the eyes have seen, but the hand says that it has not seen and that it is waiting to see. Man wants to have everything and to be able to do everything; he does not want to receive the supply of the members. This makes him poor, and the church is dragged into poverty. Authority is the riches of Christ. To receive others' function, which means to receive their authority, is to receive the riches of the whole Body. If we submit to the authority of every member, we obtain the riches of every member. If we reject the authority, we have poverty. When the eyes are illuminated, the whole body is illuminated. When the ears hear, the whole body hears.

We always think that the purpose of authority is to suppress us, smite us, and embarrass us. But God does not have this thought. We are wrong. God uses authority to fill up that which is lacking in us. God set up His authority in order to dispense His riches to us and to fill up the lack of all the weak ones. God cannot wait until we reach a certain stage or until a certain number of years have passed before He shows us something. If that were the case, we would have to pass through a countless number of dark and painful days, and a countless number of people will be led into darkness. It would truly be the blind leading the blind. How much loss God would suffer! This is why God first works thoroughly on the people who are used by Him so that when He gives them to us as our authority to help us learn submission, we can receive what we never could have otherwise received. Their riches will become our riches. If we neglect this, we might have to pass through fifty years without attaining what they have learned.

God's grace to us is twofold. On the one hand, it comes to us directly. This happens rather infrequently. On the other hand, there are indirect riches. In the church God has set brothers and sisters before us to be our authority. Through their discernments becoming our discernments we can receive their riches without going through their sufferings. In the church there is much grace which God will only give to others, not to you. Every star has its own glory. Therefore, authority is the riches of the church. Individual riches are riches for the many. To rebel is to take the way of poverty. To reject authority is to reject the way of receiving grace and riches.

DELEGATED FUNCTION BEING DEPUTY AUTHORITY

No one dares to say that he would not submit to the Lord's authority. But there is also the authority of the members in coordination that we have to submit to. We have to realize that all the members are joined together. If we do not receive help from other members, we are in rebellion. Sometimes the Lord uses one member directly. At other times, the Lord uses a member to supply another member. When the head directs the eyes to see, the whole body takes the seeing of the eyes as its own seeing because when the eyes see, the whole body sees. This delegated function, which is deputy authority, is also the authority of the Head. If any other members think that they can see for themselves, they are in rebellion. We cannot be so foolish as to think that we are almighty.

Never forget that we are just members. We need to receive the function of the other members. When we submit to the authority of the seeing function, we will have no barrier with the Head, because the supply is in the authority. Whoever has the gift has that ministry; and whoever has the ministry has the authority. No one else can see except the eyes. If we want to see, we have to submit to the authority of the eyes and receive their supply. God's appointed ministry is His authority. No one should reject it. Everyone wants to receive God's direct authority. But God wants us to submit to indirect authorities (i.e., deputy authorities) so that we may receive spiritual supply.

SUBMISSION BEING EASY WITH LIFE

For unbelievers and Israelites, submission is a difficult matter because they are not related to other unbelievers and Israelites in life. We, however, are related in life. Therefore, it is not a difficult matter to submit, for within we are all one, sharing the same life and the same Holy Spirit. The Holy Spirit directs all things. Mutual submission brings in a happy state and a lifetime of rest for us. If we take all burdens upon ourselves, it will be a tiring job. If they are distributed among the members, it will be a relaxing matter. If we are willing to be restricted by the Lord, we will have true rest. Hence, to submit to the authority of the members is a great release. Otherwise, we stand in the position of others, while causing ourselves to be under great strain. For us, submission is spontaneous, and disobedience is awkward. Why do we have to devour one another? Why do we have to criticize one another? For us these should be awkward things.

The Lord has taught us not only to learn submission in the family and in the world, but also in the Body, in the church. If we learn submission well in the Body, we will learn it well everywhere else. This is the only place to start. Hence, the church is the place of testing. It is also the place of perfection. If we do not learn well here, anything done elsewhere will not be successful. If the lesson is learned well in the church, the problem of the kingdom is solved, the problems in the world will be solved, and the problems in the universe will be solved.

In the past authority has been too objective to many, and submission also has been objective. We have tried to apply outward submission to a subjective body. Today authority has become a matter of life. In other words, it has become an inward matter. In the Body of Christ, authority and submission meet in one Body, and both have become subjective, living, and united. This is the highest expression of God's authority. Authority and submission are in one Body, and they are being brought to the highest peak. Let us be perfected here. Otherwise, there will be no way for us to go on. The place to meet authority is in the Body. The Head as the source of authority is in the church. The members who operate according to the measure of each one part, with a mutual supply between those who represent authority and those who submit to it, are also in the church. If we do not meet authority here, there is no hope for us elsewhere.

CHAPTER NINE

THE MANIFESTATION OF MAN'S REBELLION

(1)

Scripture Reading: 2 Pet. 2:10-12; Eph. 5:6; Jude 8-10; Matt. 12:34; Rom. 9:11-24

Where is man's rebellion practically manifested? First, it is manifested in words. Second, it is manifested in reasons. Third, it is manifested in the thoughts. In order to be delivered from rebellion, we must first deal with these three things. Otherwise, rebellion cannot be truly dealt with.

WORDS

Words Being the Outlet of the Heart

If a man is rebellious, his words surely will reveal rebellion. Sooner or later rebellious words will come out of his mouth, because out of the abundance of the heart the mouth speaks. In order to know authority, a man must first meet authority. If a man has not met authority, he will never be able to submit. It is useless to merely listen to messages on submission. A man must at one time meet God, and then the basis of God's authority will be established in him. When he speaks, he will know if a word of disobedience comes out. Even before the word comes out, the thought of it will give him an uneasy feeling. He will realize that he has stepped beyond his boundary and that there is a restraining within him. If a man speaks words of rebellion carelessly without any restraining within, he must be one who has never met authority. It is much easier for a man to speak in rebellion than to act in rebellion.

The tongue is the thing that is the hardest to tame. Therefore, when a man rebels against authority, the tongue will show it immediately. Perhaps one agrees with you in your presence, but when the back is turned reviling words will come out. No words may be spoken up front, but the mouth is filled with words when the back is turned. This is because the mouth is so available. Everyone in the world today is rebellious. Mostly people pay lip service and submit outwardly. But in the church there should not be just outward submission; all submission should come from the heart. If you want to know whether or not a man is submissive in heart, see if he is submissive in words. God requires a submission of the heart from us. We have to meet God's authority or the problem will explode sooner or later.

Eve Adding Carelessly to God's Word

When Eve was tempted in Genesis 3, she added a few words: "Neither shall ye touch it" (v. 3). We have to realize the seriousness of this matter. If man knows God's authority, he will not dare add to God's word. The word of God is clear enough. "Of every tree of the garden thou mayest freely eat: but of the tree of the knowledge of good and evil, thou shalt not eat of it" (2:16-17). God did not say, "Neither shall ye touch it." Those words were added by Eve. Whoever changes God's word by adding to or deleting from it proves that he has never met authority. Such a one is surely rebellious and unlearned. If a government sends a person as a representative to speak a word at a certain place, that person must remember precisely the words that he is to speak. He must not add anything else to the words. Although Eve saw God every day, she did not know authority. She spoke carelessly, thinking that it was all right to say a few words more or less. If a mortal man serving a mortal master would not dare to add to or delete from his master's words, how much more should we who serve God be careful in doing the same? If a man speaks carelessly, it proves that he is a rebellious one.

Ham Exposing His Father's Failure

Look at the behavior of Ham, the son of Noah. When he saw the nakedness of his father, he went out to tell Shem and Japheth (9:20-22). A person who is not submissive in heart always likes to see authority in failure. Ham found the opportunity to expose his father's mistakes. This proves that he was one who did not submit to his father's authority. Previously, he submitted through pressure. When he saw his father's mistake, he exposed it to his two brothers. Many brothers criticize others and delight in tearing them down because of a lack of love (1 Cor. 13:4-5). With Ham there was not just a lack of love, but a lack of submission. It was a manifestation of rebellion.

Miriam and Aaron's Reviling of Moses

In Numbers 12 Miriam and Aaron spoke against Moses. They mixed up family affairs with the work. In God's calling Moses was singled out; Miriam and Aaron were only the helpers. This was God's decision. The disobedience of these two was also manifested in words. If we know authority, many mouths will be shut and many problems will be prevented. Once we meet authority, many natural problems are gone. Miriam's words did not seem to be an overstepping. She only said, "Has Jehovah indeed spoken only through Moses? Has he not spoken through us also?" (v. 2). But God understood that as reviling (v. 8). Perhaps there were many words which they had not spoken. Perhaps what was revealed was only the tip of the iceberg, a tenth of all that was there. Perhaps ninety percent was still hidden. As long as there is a spirit of rebellion in man, God will detect it no matter how many nice words he speaks. Rebellion is manifested in words. A rebellious word speaks of rebellion no matter whether it is strong or weak.

The Company of Korah Attacking Moses

In Numbers 16 when the company of Korah and the 250 leaders rebelled, the manifestation was all the more in words. Whatever they had in their heart they spoke. They even broke out in open rebuke. Although Miriam reviled, she did so in a reserved way, and as such there was still the possibility of recovery. But the company of Korah had no restraint. Everything spilled over like a flood. Even rebellion has degrees. Some have more of a sense of shame, and they can be recovered. But those who have shaken off all restraints, who are completely unchecked, open the gates of Hades for themselves, and Hades swallows them up. Not only did the company of Korah speak in an evil way; they attacked in an open way. It was so serious that Moses had to fall on his face. How serious were such words: You take too much upon you. Why are you lifting yourselves up above the congregation of the Lord? We only recognize Jehovah in our midst. The whole congregation is holy. We do not recognize your authority. You are taking too much upon yourselves. *Here we see that whoever listens only to God's direct authority, but refuses His deputy authority, is in the principle of rebellion.*

If a man submits to authority, surely he will restrict his mouth. He will not be careless. In Acts 23 Paul was being tried. As an apostle and prophet he spoke in the position of a prophet to Ananias the high priest: "God is going to strike you, you whitewashed wall" (v. 3). But at the same time Paul was a Jew. When he heard that Ananias was the high priest, he immediately softened and said, "'You shall not speak evilly of the ruler of your people'" (v. 5). How careful he was in his words, and how much he restricted his mouth.

Rebellion Being Related to
the Walking after the Lust in the Flesh

Man's rebellion is especially related to the indulgence of the flesh. In 2 Peter 2:10 the flesh and the lust were first mentioned, then those who despise lordship. The expression of this despising of lordship is shown in reviling words, words of rebellion.

Particular kinds of people live among those who are of their own kind; they have communication with their kind of people. Rebellious ones always accompany those who walk after the flesh. They are also the ones who accompany those who indulge in the lust of uncleanness and who despise lordship. In God's eyes, walking after the flesh, indulging in lust, and despising lordship are all the same thing. Such ones are presumptuous, self-willed, and not afraid of speaking evil of dignities. But those who know God are fearful on their behalf. The mouth has a lust, which is to speak evil words.

If we know God, we will be repentant and remorseful, because we will realize how much God hates this. The angels were under those with lordship at one time. For this reason, they dare not revile them with evil words. They dare not deal with a lawless spirit by lawless means. Therefore, if we live before God, we cannot revile others with reviling words. Please notice that it is possible to speak reviling words even in our prayers. David could say that Saul was God's anointed. This proves that he was one who kept the proper position. The power of Satan is established upon lawlessness, while the angels are those that would not overstep their position. Peter used this as an example to show us that since the angels in the heavens are like this, we should be like that even more (v. 11).

There are only two things that cause a Christian to lose his power. One is sin, and the other is speaking evil of those above him. The more evil speaking, the more power is lost. If a man's lack of submission is in his heart only, without corresponding utterances from his mouth, his power will not be lost as fast. The effect of speaking is much more serious than we can imagine.

To God, man's thoughts and conduct are the same. As long as there is a thought, a sin is committed. However, Matthew 12:34-37 also says that out of the abundance of the heart the mouth speaks. In the day of judgment, we will be judged righteous or sinful according to the words we have spoken. This shows us that there is a difference between words and thoughts. If there are no words, there is still the possibility of covering up. But if the words come out, everything is thrown into the open. For this reason, disobedience in heart is a little better than openly speaking with the mouth. Today Christians lose their power through their mouth in no less measure than they lose it through their conduct. Actually, more is lost through the mouth. All rebellious ones have trouble with their speaking. Hence, if a man cannot restrict himself in words, he cannot restrict himself in anything.

God Rebuking the Rebellious Ones
with the Strongest Words

Look again at 2 Peter 2:12, which says, "But these, like

animals without reason, born natural for capture and destruction..." This is the strongest word in the Bible. There is no word of rebuke more serious than this. Why does the Bible rebuke these ones as animals? It is because these ones have no feelings. Authority is the most central thing in the Bible. Hence, to God reviling is the most serious of all sins. The mouth cannot speak lightly. As soon as a man meets God, his mouth will be restricted, and there will be a fear of reviling dignities. Once we meet authority, there will be a sense of authority in us, in the same way that there will be a sense of sin once we meet the Lord.

Problems in the Church Arising Frequently from Reviling Words

The oneness and the power of the church are broken through man's careless words. Today the majority of the problems in the church come from evil speakings. Only a minority come from real difficulties. The majority of the sins in the world also come from lies. If evil words are stopped in the church, the majority of our problems will be reduced. We need to repent before the Lord and ask for His forgiveness. Evil speaking needs a thorough termination in the church. Out of one spring there cannot issue two kinds of water. Out of one mouth there cannot issue words of love and words of reviling. May God set a watchman upon our mouth, and not only upon our mouth, but also upon our heart so that all words and thoughts of reviling would be stopped. May evil speaking depart from among us from this day forward.

REASONS

Reviling Words Being from Reasons

Man's rebellion is manifested in words, reasons, and thoughts. If a man does not know authority, there will be reviling words. But these words come from reasons. Man speaks because he thinks he has a reason. Ham thought that he had a reason to revile Noah because he was naked. Miriam's word concerning Moses marrying an Ethiopian woman was a fact; she had a reason. However, those who submit to authority and live under authority do not live in their reasons. Korah's company and the 250 leaders said that Moses and Aaron should not put themselves above the others because the whole congregation was holy and Jehovah was in their midst. Again, their rebellion had a reason behind it. Reviling words often come from reasons. Dathan and Abiram had even more reasons. They charged that Moses had not brought them into the land flowing with milk and honey, that he had not given them the inheritance of fields and vineyards, but rather that they were still in the wilderness. They charged that Moses was just covering up their eyes, saying, "Will you put out the eyes of these men?" (Num. 16:14). This meant that their eyes were very clear. The more they thought, the more reason they had. Reason cannot stand thinking. The more thinking there is, the more reasons are stirred up. In the world everyone lives in reasons. What difference is there between us and the worldly people if we also live in reasons?

Being Delivered from Reasons to Follow the Lord

Indeed we need to put out our eyes and follow the Lord without reason. Are our lives based upon reasons or upon authority? Many become blind when they are struck by the Lord's light. Although they have eyes, it is as if they have none. Once the light comes, all reasons are gone. Once Paul was enlightened on the way to Damascus, he became truly blind. From then on he did not care for reasons (Acts 9:3, 8). Moses' eyes were not put out, but he was like a man without eyes. It was not that he had no reasons; he knew many reasons. But all the reasons were under him because he submitted to God. Those who submit to authority do not act by sight. A servant of the Lord must be blind. He must be delivered from a life of reasons. Reasoning in the heart is the first cause of rebellion. Hence, if we do not deal thoroughly with reasons, it is impossible to stop the words. If we are not delivered from reasons, they will issue forth in reviling words sooner or later.

How difficult it is to be delivered from a life of reason. We are rational beings. How can it be possible for us to not reason with God? This is a very difficult point. We reason continually from our youth. From the time before we believed in the Lord even until now, the basic principle of our living has been in reasoning. What can cause us to stop now? Requiring us to do so will take our flesh-life to the gallows! There are two kinds of Christians: one living on the level of reason and the other living on the level of authority. We should submit as soon as there is a command. On which level are we living? When God has a command, do we consider a little and submit when there are sufficient reasons and not submit when there are insufficient reasons? This is the expression of the tree of the knowledge of good and evil. The fruit of the tree of the knowledge of good and evil causes us not only to discern things in ourselves, but to discern things established by God as well. All these have to pass through our reasons and judgments. We can reason for God and even make judgments for God, but this is the principle of Satan. Satan wants to be equal with God. Those who know God only have submission; there is no reason with them. The two never mingle together. If a man wants to learn submission, he has to throw away reasons. Either he lives by God's authority or he lives by reasons. He cannot have both. The Lord Jesus lived a life on earth that was completely beyond reason. What reason was there for the insults, tortures, and crucifixion that He suffered? He, nevertheless, submitted under God's authority. He did not care for any reason. He was only responsible for submission. He did not ask for anything else. How simple is the man who lives under authority! But how complicated is the man who lives in reasons! The birds in the air and the lilies in the field live a simple life. The more a person lives under authority, the simpler his life will become.

God Never Reasoning

In Romans 9 Paul tried to prove to the Jews that God has called the Gentiles also. He said that not all of the seed of Abraham were chosen; only Isaac was chosen. And not all of the seed of Isaac were chosen; God chose only Jacob. Since everything is of God's choice, can God not choose the Gentiles as well? God will have mercy on whomever He will have mercy, and will have compassion on whomever He will have compassion. Humanly speaking, God loved the wicked Jacob, while He hated the honest Esau. He also hardened Pharaoh. Is He then unfair? We have to realize that God sits on His throne of glory, and man is under His authority. Who are we but humble mortals, nothing but dust. How can we reason with God?

He is God. He has the authority to do things. We cannot follow God on the one hand, while forcing Him to listen to our reason on the other hand. If we want to serve Him, we must give up all reasons. Every person who has met the Lord has to throw away all his reasons. We can only stand on the position of submission. We cannot stand on the position of interference, attempting to act as God's counselor. God says that He will have mercy on whomever He will have mercy (9:15). How precious is the word "will have." We have to worship Him for this. God does not reason at all. God chooses to do this. He delights in doing this. He is the God of glory. Paul went on to say, "So then it is not of him who wills, nor of him who runs, but of God who shows mercy" (v. 16). God said of Pharaoh, "For this very thing I have raised you up, that I might show in you My power" (v. 17). Moreover, He said that "He hardens whom He wills" (v. 18). To harden does not mean to cause to sin. It means to "give one up" as recorded in 1:26. Up to this point Paul anticipated that there would be more reasonings, such as, "Why does He still find fault? For who withstands His will?" (9:19). These reasons are very valid. Many will agree with them. Paul also knew that they were quite reasonable and sensible, but he retorted, "But rather, O man, who are you who answer back to God? Shall the thing molded say to him who molded it, Why did you make me thus?" (v. 20). Paul did not counter the reasons. Rather he asked, "Who are you?" Paul did not ask what kind of words these are. He asked rather what kind of person would dare reply against God. When God exercises His authority, He does not have to discuss it with us. He does not need our consent. All He asks is our submission to Him. As long as we say, "This is God's doing," everything will be fine.

Man is constantly trying to reason. But please consider whether or not our salvation had any reason behind it. There was absolutely no reason for our salvation. We did not will, nor did we run. But we were saved. This is the most unreasonable thing. But God will have mercy on whom He will have mercy. Out of the clay, the potter can make one vessel to honor and another to dishonor. There is only the question of authority. There is no question of reason. The basic problem with man today is that he is still under the principle of the knowledge of good and evil, the principle of reasoning. If the Bible reasoned out everything, then we could be justified in reasoning out everything. But in Romans 9 God opened up a special window from heaven to shine on us. He did not reason with us. He only asked, "Who are you?"

Seeing God's Glory Delivering Us from Reasons

It is not easy for man to be delivered from evil speaking. But it is more difficult for man to be delivered from reason. When I was young, I was always bothered by God's unreasonable acts. Later, when I read Romans 9, I touched God's authority for the first time. I began to see who I am. I am His creature. My most reasonable words are but stubbornness before Him. The God who is far above all is unapproachable in His glory. If we would see only a millionth part of His glory, we would bow down and cast off all our reasons. Only those who live far off can be proud, and only those who live in darkness can abide in reasons. No one in the whole world can see himself in his own torchlight. Only when the Lord grants us a little light and reveals a little of His glory to us will we fall down as dead, just like the apostle John (Rev. 1:16-17).

May God be merciful to us that we would see how unworthy and lowly a person we are. How dare we argue with God? When the queen of the south came to visit Solomon and he revealed a little of his glory to her, there was no more spirit left in her. But there is One who is greater than Solomon. Is there any reason in me that cannot be given up? Adam sinned because he ate of the fruit of the tree of the knowledge of good and evil. From then on, reason became rooted in man's very being. But if God would reveal just a little of His glory to us, we would see that we are but a dead dog and a lump of clay. All our reasons would vanish in His glory. The more a person lives in glory, the less he will reason. However, the more you see a person reason, the more you know that he has never seen glory.

During these years I have found out one thing—God's work is never according to reasons. Even if I do not understand what He is doing, I still have to worship Him because I am His servant. If everything that He does is understood and realized by me, I might as well be the one to sit on the throne. Once I see that He is far above me, that only He is the Most High One, and that I should bow down in the dust, all reasons will disappear from me. From this day forward, authority only is the fact, not reasons, rights, and wrongs. Those who know God surely know themselves, and once a person knows himself, all reasons are removed.

The way to know God is by submission. Everyone who lives in reason does not know God. Only those who willingly submit to authority can truly know God. All of the knowledge of good and evil that we inherited from Adam must be removed. Then our submission will be very easy.

"I Am Jehovah" Being the Reason

Every time the Lord commanded the Israelites to do something in Leviticus 18—22, He inserted the words, "I am Jehovah," in between the commands. There is not even the word *because*. I speak this way, for I am Jehovah. There need be no other reason. "I am Jehovah" is the reason. If we see this, we will not live by reason from this day on. We have to say to God, "In the past I lived by my thoughts and reasons. Today I bow down and worship You. As long as it is of You, it is enough for me. I will worship You." When Paul was struck down on the way to Damascus, all reasons vanished from him. Once light shines in, a person falls down. The first word that came out of Paul's mouth was, "What shall I do, Lord?" (Acts 22:10). Immediately, he became obedient. Those who know God do not reason. When the light judges, the reason disappears.

For man to reason with God is for him to say that God's work requires our consent. This is the thought of the most foolish. God does not have to tell us the reason for anything He does. God's way is higher than our way. If we pulled God down to the level of reason, we would have God no longer, because He would be no different from us. If we reason, there will be no more worship. When submission goes, a lack of worship follows. When this happens, the self becomes the judge of God and even becomes God. What difference then is there between the clay and the potter? Will the potter have to ask permission from the clay to do anything? May God's glory be revealed so that all our reasons cease.

CHAPTER TEN

THE MANIFESTATION OF MAN'S REBELLION

(2)

Scripture Reading: 2 Cor. 10:4-6

THOUGHTS

The Relationship
between Reasons and Thoughts

Not only is man's rebellion manifested in his words and reasons; it is manifested in his thoughts as well. Man speaks rebellious words because he has rebellious reasons. But reasons are manifested in one's thoughts. Therefore, thought is the center of man's rebellion.

Second Corinthians 10:4-6 is one of the most important passages in the Bible, because it especially points out which part of a man should submit to Christ. Verse 5 speaks of taking "captive every thought unto the obedience of Christ." Man's rebellion is a rebellion of thought. Paul said that we have to overthrow the strongholds, the reasonings, and every high thing rising up against the knowledge of God. Man uses reasonings to build a fortress around his thoughts. This reasoning must be overthrown, and the thoughts must be taken captive. Discard the reasons, but take back the thoughts. Today reason is man's fortress, and thoughts are imprisoned in it. Spiritual warfare involves storming this fortress and recapturing the thoughts. It is impossible for man's thoughts to submit to God without overthrowing reasons. All reasonings frustrate man from knowing God. The "high things" are like tall buildings. In God's eyes man's reasons are a tall building, a big obstruction along the way of knowing God. Once a man reasons, his thoughts are surrounded; they can no longer submit to God. Submission is a matter of the thoughts. If reasons are manifested, they become words. If reasons are hidden, they encircle the thoughts, and submission becomes impossible. Paul was not dealing with reasonings by reasoning. Man's reasonings are so serious that they cannot be dealt with except by battle. The mind with its reasonings can only be dealt with by spiritual armor, by God's power. This is a battle between God and us. We have become God's opponent. Man's reasoning mind is inherited from the tree of the knowledge of good and evil. It is hard to imagine how much trouble this mind gives to God. Satan binds us through different kinds of reasons so that we become the prisoner to reasons, unable to be gained by God, and so we also become God's enemy.

Genesis 3 is a picture of 2 Corinthians 10. Satan reasoned with Eve. When Eve saw that the fruit of the tree was good for food, she also reasoned. She disobeyed God for a reason. Once reason comes, man's thoughts are stuck in it. Reasons and thoughts go together. Reason preys on thoughts. Once the thoughts are captured, man will no longer be able to submit to Christ. If we want to submit to God, we must touch God's authority and break through all the strongholds of reasons.

Taking the Thoughts Captive

In the Greek New Testament, the word for *thought* is *noema*. This Greek word is used six times in the New Testament, in Philippians 4:7; 2 Corinthians 2:11; 3:14; 4:4; 10:5; and 11:3. The word is rightly translated as "thought," which means propositions of the heart. The heart is the organ, and the propositions are its activities. They are the product of man's mind. Man asserts himself through the liberty of opinions and propositions. In order to protect his liberty, all of his propositions must be justified as being good and correct. They must not be contended with. Therefore, he has to surround them with many reasons. A man refuses to believe in the Lord usually because of one or two reasons with which he surrounds himself as strongholds. For example, some say that they will believe when they get old, that they do not see good examples in Christians who have believed, or that they will have to wait until their parents die before they can believe. There are also many reasons for Christians not to love the Lord. Students say that they are too busy with their schoolwork. Businessmen say that they are too occupied with their businesses or that they do not feel well physically. If God does not break through these strongholds, man will never be liberated. Satan uses reasons as strongholds to keep man in. Man is outwardly surrounded by these fortresses of reasons. By himself man cannot break through to freedom. Submission to Christ is possible only through the authority of God that captures the thoughts and makes them God's slaves.

For man to know authority, he must first break down reasons. When man sees God as He is presented in Romans 9, all reasons are shattered. When Satan's stronghold is torn down, there is no more reason, and the thoughts are taken captive unto the obedience of Christ. It is not enough for man to meet authority in his speaking. It is not enough to remove all reasons. His thoughts must be captured unto the obedience of Christ. Only when his thoughts are captured can man truly submit to Christ.

To discern whether or not a man has met authority, we need to see if such a one has been dealt with in speaking, in reasons, and in opinions. Once a man has confronted authority, his tongue will not be that careless, his reasonings will not be that bold, and deeper still, his opinions will not be exercised. An ordinary man has many opinions, and he uses many outward reasons to fortify his opinions. A day must come when God's authority comes in to remove the strongholds that Satan has set up through reasons and to capture the thoughts of man, making him a willing slave of God who subjects himself to Christ without any opinion. Only then will there be a thorough salvation.

A person who has never met authority always wants to be God's counselor. His thoughts are not captured by God. When he goes to a place, the first thought that occurs to him is to "improve." When thoughts are not disciplined, there are many reasons and no brokenness is seen. Therefore, our

thoughts have to be cut so deeply that they are captured back
to God. Only then can we see the authority of God. Only then
will we not dare to hide under our reasons and express our
opinions carelessly.

There often seem to be two persons in the whole world
who know everything—one is God and the other is myself.
I am the counselor. I know everything. When this is the case,
it clearly shows that the thoughts are not captured and that
there is no knowledge of authority. A person whose stronghold
of reasons has been broken by God's authority will have his
thoughts captured by God; he can submit to Christ and be
free from expressing opinions. In fact, he will not be inter-
ested in expressing his opinions. His thoughts will become
the slaves of God, and he will no longer be a free man. The
natural freedom is a prey for Satan. Such freedom has to be
given up. We would only be obedient ones. There are only
two ways in which man's thoughts can be used. One is being
under the control of reasons, and the other is being under
the control of Christ's authority. Actually, there is no such
thing as freedom of choice in the whole world. We are
captured either by reasons or by the Lord. We are either
Satan's slaves or God's slaves.

To discern whether or not a brother has met authority, we
first need to find out whether he has rebellious words; second,
we need to find out whether or not he reasons before God;
and third, whether or not he expresses opinions. Before the
Lord we must take care of the shattering of our reasons, but
this is only the negative aspect. The reasons have to be
shattered in order that the thoughts may be taken captive
unto the obedience of Christ and no longer dare express their
own opinions. Formerly, I gave many reasons based on my own
opinions. Today all my reasons are gone. I owe submission to
whoever has captured me. A captive has no freedom. Even if
he expresses an opinion, it is useless. A captive cannot present
his own opinions. He can only receive opinions. It is the same
way when we are taken captive by the Lord. We no longer
express opinions or suggestions. Instead, we only take God's
opinion.

A Warning to the Opinionated Ones

Paul

Paul was an intelligent, able, wise, and sensible person. He was capable and confident in his work, and served God with his own zeal. When he was on his way to Damascus with a company of men to lay hold of Christians, he suddenly met a great light, which struck him to the ground. In that moment all of his opinions and methods were gone. All his capabilities were shattered. He did not go back to Tarsus, nor did he go back to Jerusalem. Not only was his trip to Damascus thrown away; all of his reasons were thrown away as well. When many encounter difficulties, they turn another direction. If one way is blocked, they try another way. All the while they still journey according to their own methods and opinions. Many are so foolish that they do not fall even when they are struck by God. They are only struck by God in the event. They are not struck by God in their reason; their thoughts are still present. Many have been cut off from their way to Damascus, but they still find a way to Tarsus or to Jerusalem. But once Paul was struck, everything was over. Nothing more needed to be said. Nothing more needed to be considered. He did not know anything anymore. He asked the Lord, "What shall I do, Lord?" Here was a man who was submissive from the heart. His thoughts were captured by the Lord. Saul had been an outstanding and distinguished person everywhere he went, but when he met the authority of God, all of his opinions were gone. The biggest mark of a person who has met God is the absence of prejudice and cleverness. We have to ask for God's mercy that we would be simple in the light. He who meets God's authority will fall before God's face and spontaneously have no more opinions. Paul said that he had been captured by God to be His prisoner. Now is not the time for us to express opinions. Our place is just to listen and submit.

King Saul

Saul was rejected by God, not for theft but for offering a sacrifice to God of sheep and oxen that he assumed were the best. This was his opinion. He was trying to please God by his own thoughts. His thoughts were not captured, and he was thus rejected by God. One cannot say that Saul was not zealous in his service to God. He did not lie. They were the best of the sheep and the oxen. The problem, however, was that he made a decision based on his own opinion (1 Sam. 15). A servant of God cannot express his own opinion; he can only carry out God's will. We should have only one desire: "What shall I do, Lord?" If this is not our attitude, we are completely wrong. To obey is better than sacrifice. There is no place for man to express his opinion before God. When King Saul saw so many fat sheep and oxen, he wanted to keep some for offerings. His heart was for God, but his obedience was short. Having a heart for God cannot replace the words, "I dare not say anything." And the offerings of the fat cannot replace an attitude of "having no voice" before the Lord. God commanded that all the Amalekites with their sheep and oxen be completely destroyed, but Saul was unwilling to do it. Later, the Amalekites killed him, and his reign was stopped. Whoever comes up with a proposal to save the Amalekites will be killed by the Amalekites in the end.

Nadab and Abihu

Nadab and Abihu were also rebellious in the matter of sacrifice. They did not submit to the authority of their father, but instead made a proposal out of their own initiative. They committed the sin of offending God. It was a sin of offering strange fire, a matter of overstepping God's minister. Although they did not say anything or murmur any reasonings, they burned incense by their own will and according to their own feeling. They thought that this kind of service was a good thing. If they were wrong, they thought that it was but a mistake in service. To them it was not a great sin. But it turned out that they were immediately rejected by God and immediately died.

The Testimony of the Kingdom
Made Possible Only through Submission

God does not check on our zeal for the gospel or our

willingness to suffer; He checks to see whether or not we are obedient. Refraining from opinion, stopping all reasonings, ceasing all evil speaking, and submitting to God completely are the beginning of the kingdom. This will be a day of glory, the day that God has been waiting for since the foundation of the earth. God has a Firstborn who has already submitted, who is the firstfruit. Yet God is waiting for all the sons to be conformed identically to the Son. If there is a church on earth that truly submits to God's authority, there will be the testimony of the kingdom, and Satan will be defeated. Satan is not afraid of our work. As long as we stand on the principle of rebellion and act independently by our own will, Satan will laugh in secret.

According to the law of Moses, the ark should have been borne by the Levites. But when the Philistines sent the ark back to the Israelites, they did so with an oxcart. When David desired to receive the ark into the city of David, he did not seek the will of God. Rather, he made his own proposal and pulled the ark by the oxen. When the oxen stumbled, the ark fell, and Uzzah stretched forth his hand to uphold it. Immediately, he was smitten by God and died. Even if the ark did not fall, it was at most on an oxcart; it was not on the shoulders of the Levites. When the Levites lifted the ark across the Jordan, the waves were high. Yet the ark was in peace. This tells us one thing: God does not like man's proposals. Man must forever be submissive to God. Only when God empties us completely can His will be done unhindered. If we come with our human opinions, service to God will never have a way. Everything is done through God's ruling, not man's scheming. Man's opinion must be thoroughly dismantled. His thoughts must be shut up; they must be forbidden from making suggestions. In the past there was freedom in living by the self. But when the thoughts are captured, there is no more freedom. As a result we can be obedient to Christ and have the true freedom, a freedom that is in the Lord.

Second Corinthians 10:6 says, "We are ready to punish all disobedience when your obedience is fulfilled." Only when the thoughts are captured can obedience be fulfilled. Everyone who can still maneuver and express opinions before God does not have his obedience fulfilled. The Lord is ready. When our obedience is fulfilled, He will rise up to avenge the disobedient ones. If we would thoroughly turn around and be fearful of our own opinions and proposals, our obedience will be fulfilled, and God will manifest His authority on earth today. If the church cannot be submissive, much less can the world be submissive. If the church is not submissive, it is vain to hope for others to submit to the gospel. Only with a submissive church can there be a submissive response to the gospel. All of us have to learn to be restricted. Our mouths have to be disciplined to stop speaking. Our minds have to be disciplined to stop reasoning. Our hearts have to be disciplined to stop proposing. If we do this, a way of glory will be before us, and God will manifest His authority on earth.

CHAPTER ELEVEN

THE PROPER LIMIT
OF SUBMISSION TO AUTHORITY

Scripture Reading: Heb. 11:23; Exo. 1:17; Dan. 3:17-18; 6:10;
Matt. 2:13; Acts 5:29

SUBMISSION BEING ABSOLUTE,
BUT OBEDIENCE BEING RELATIVE

Submission is a matter of attitude, but obedience is a
matter of conduct. Acts 4:19 says, "But Peter and John
answered and said to them, Whether it is right in the sight
of God to listen to you rather than to God, you judge." The
apostles, however, were not rebellious in their spirit; they
were still submitting to all those who were in authority.
Obedience is not absolute. Some authorities we have to obey,
but others we cannot obey. The latter include those who touch
on basic matters of the Christian faith, such as our belief in
the Lord and the liberty of preaching the gospel. A son can
say anything to his father. But there cannot be any attitude
of rebellion. Our submission should always be absolute. In
some matters we can be obedient at the same time that we
are submissive. In other matters we cannot be obedient, but
we still have to remain submissive. All these are a matter of
attitude.

Acts 15 is an example of a church conference. In a conference we can suggest or debate. But when the decision is
reached, everyone should be submissive.

THE LIMIT OF OBEYING THE DEPUTY AUTHORITY

If there are parents who force their children to stop
attending church meetings, the children should be submissive
in their attitude, but they must not obey. This is like the

apostles preaching the gospel. When the Jewish synagogue stopped them, they were submissive in their attitude, but in practice they went on according to the commission of the Lord. They chose to preach the gospel rather than be restricted by the synagogue. It was not a defiance with quarrels and shouting, but a defiance with calmness. At any rate, there must never be any attitude of stubbornness or words of contradiction against those in authority. Once a man meets authority, he becomes soft and pliant. The submission of a person in heart, attitude, and words must be absolute. There must not be any stubbornness or rebellion.

When the deputy authority (the one representing God's authority) clashes with the direct authority (God), one must be submissive to the deputy authority but must not be obedient to it. We will summarize the matter in three points:

(1) Obedience is a matter of conduct; it is relative. Submission is a matter of attitude; it is absolute.

(2) Only God is the object of unlimited submission. Man, who is less than God, should only receive limited submission.

(3) If the deputy authority gives an order that is obviously contrary to God's order, we can only submit; we cannot obey. We must submit only to the authority of God. We do not obey the orders that are contrary to God.

If parents ask their children to go to places that the children do not like to go to, and if there is no sin involved in the matter, we have a borderline case. Submission is absolute. But obedience is another matter. If your parents force you to go, then you have no choice but to go. But if they do not force you to do it, you do not have to go. If all children have this attitude, God will release them in their environments.

EXAMPLES IN THE BIBLE

(1) The midwives and the mother of Moses disobeyed the order of Pharaoh so that the life of Moses could be preserved. The Bible calls them women of faith.

(2) The three friends of Daniel did not worship the golden image of King Nebuchadnezzar. They disobeyed the order of the king, yet they submitted to the king's burning.

(3) Daniel defied the decree in order to pray to God, yet he submitted to the king's judgment to be thrown into the lion's den.

(4) Joseph escaped with the Lord Jesus to Egypt to avoid the killing by King Herod.

(5) Peter went contrary to the charge of those in the synagogue and preached the gospel. He also said that it was right to obey God rather than men. Yet he submitted to the rulers' chains and imprisonment.

DEFINITE MARKS OF SUBMISSION TO AUTHORITY

How do we know if a person is one who submits to authority? Here are a few marks:

(1) As soon as a person meets authority, he will look for authority everywhere. The church is the organ for the training of Christian submission to authority. In the whole world there is no such thing as submission. But a Christian must learn submission. He must, moreover, submit from the heart, not just in an outward way. Once a person learns submission, he will look for authority wherever he goes.

(2) Once a man meets God's authority, he will soften, wither, and weaken. This is because he has become fearful of making mistakes; he is a truly soft person.

(3) Those who have met authority will not like to be the authority. They will have no desire or interest to be an authority. They have no joy in giving opinions or in controlling others. Those who submit to authority are always afraid of making mistakes. But many love to be God's counselors. Only those who do not know authority love to be the authority.

(4) Those who have met authority will have their mouths shut. They will be restricted. They will not dare to speak carelessly, because they have the consciousness of authority with them.

(5) If a man has met authority, any transgression in others will be detected by him immediately. He will see through many lawlessnesses and realize many rebellions. He will then come to know that the principle of lawlessness abounds everywhere, in the world as well as in the church. Only those who have met authority can lead others to learn submission.

Only when the brothers and sisters are submissive to authority will the church have a testimony and a way on earth.

UPHOLDING THE ORDER OF AUTHORITY
DEPENDING ON THE KNOWLEDGE OF AUTHORITY

If a man has not met authority and does not know the principle of submission to authority, he cannot bring others into the way of submission and authority. If you put two dogs together, you cannot make one the authority and make the other submit to authority. This is useless. If a man meets authority, everything is solved. Once he violates authority, he will realize that he has violated God. If a man has not seen authority, it is useless to point out his mistakes. When such a situation occurs, we have to withdraw and take care lest we fall into the same realm of rebellion.

MARTIN LUTHER AND LEAVING THE DENOMINATIONS

It was right for Martin Luther to rise up to speak for the basic principle of justification by faith. It is also right for us to leave the denominations to stand as the testimony of oneness in the local church. Since we have seen the glory of Christ and the Body of Christ, we cannot have any other name apart from the name of the Lord. The Lord's name is of foremost importance. Why is salvation not only through the blood of Christ but also through the name of the Lord? This is because the Lord's name means resurrection and ascension. God has only one way of salvation, and He has placed this under the name of the Lord. In baptism we are baptized into the name of the Lord, and our meeting together is in the name of the Lord. Therefore, the cross and the blood alone cannot solve the problem of denominations. If a man sees the glory of ascension, he cannot insist on any name other than that of the Lord's. We can only exalt the Lord's name. There cannot be any other name. Today's denominational organizations are overthrowing the Lord's glory. This is a blasphemy to the Lord.

LIFE AND AUTHORITY

The church is maintained by two things: life and authority.

The life is for us to submit to authority. The difficulties in the church seldom arise from disobedience. They mainly arise from an unwillingness to submit. The principle of our life is that of submission, in the same way that the principle of the bird life is to fly in the air, and the principle of the fish life is to swim in the water. The way of oneness in Ephesians 4 seems far off now. But if men meet authority, the way is not far away. All of the saints may have differences of opinion, but there is no rebellion. The submission is from the heart. Then we will all arrive at the oneness of the faith. Today the life is here, and the principle of life is also opened to us. If the Lord is merciful to us, we will be able to take up this way quickly. Today life is not only for us to deal with sin. That is only the negative aspect. Life is also for submission. This is more crucial, and is the positive aspect of it. Once the spirit of rebellion departs from us, the spirit of submission will be recovered, and the situation in Ephesians 4 will be manifested before our eyes. If all the churches take the way of submission, these glorious facts will unfold before our eyes.

PART TWO

HOW TO BE
GOD'S DEPUTY AUTHORITY

CHAPTER TWELVE

THE KIND OF PERSON
GOD USES TO BE HIS DEPUTY AUTHORITY

SUBMISSION TO DEPUTY AUTHORITY
AND BEING A DEPUTY AUTHORITY

God's children must learn to know authority and find out to whom they should submit. Wherever we go, the first thing we should ask is whose authority should we be under. As soon as we move to a place, we should not expect to be the master, asking others to submit to us. Instead, we should be like the centurion, who told the Lord Jesus, "For I also am a man under authority, having soldiers under me" (Matt. 8:9). Here was a man who truly knew authority. He could submit to authority; therefore, he was able to be a deputy authority himself. We have said that God upholds and maintains the whole universe with His authority. He also begets His children with His authority (John 1:12) and binds them together with His authority. Therefore, if a man is independent, individualistic, and free from any God-appointed deputy authority, he is an outsider as far as God's administration over the whole universe is concerned. He cannot get along with other children of God, and as such, he cannot accomplish God's work on earth today. God has established deputy authorities in the church; the church is built up and maintained by the authority of God. For this reason every child of God should look for the authority to whom he should submit so that he can coordinate with others in a proper way. Unfortunately, many people have failed in this point.

If we do not know the object of our faith, we cannot believe in anything. If we do not know the object of our love, we cannot love anyone. If we want a person to believe in something, we first must show him the object of his faith. If we want a person to love someone, we first must show him the object of his love. In the same way, if we do not know the object of our submission, we will not know how to submit. In order to teach a person submission, we first must let him know the person to whom he should submit. There are many deputy authorities in the church to whom we should render submission. When we submit to them, we are submitting to God. Many people can preach submission, but they themselves cannot submit to any authority. We must be a person who submits to authority before we can be a deputy authority ourselves. Moreover, we cannot submit only to those whom we love; we have to learn to submit to all authorities over us. Even the policeman on the street is an object of our submission.

THE NEED TO ENCOUNTER AUTHORITY IN A THOROUGH WAY

There are many authorities in the church. They are over you, and you have to learn to submit to all of them. You have to learn to face all kinds of authority, and you must recognize authority in others. Once you encounter authority in a person, you have to learn to submit to that person immediately. You should not weigh him carefully and then decide if you should submit to him. If you consider whether or not a person is worthy of submission before you submit to him, you have only encountered the person himself; you have not encountered authority itself. If a man has not met authority, he can never be a deputy authority himself. If a man does not know how to submit to authority, he cannot be God's deputy authority. Unless a man first deals with rebellion in himself, he does not know how to be an authority. Unless we first judge the sin of rebellion in us, we cannot know what submission is. God's children should not be unorganized and tangled yarn or a mob of undisciplined people. If there is no testimony of submission among God's children, there will be no church, and there will be no ministry and no work. We must realize that this is a grave problem. We must have a very serious dealing before the Lord, and must encounter the matter of authority in a thorough way. We have to learn to submit to one another, and we must learn to submit to deputy authorities. Only after that can we begin to learn to be a deputy authority.

Three Requirements for Deputy Authorities

Today we will consider the kind of persons God uses to be His deputy authorities. In order to be God's deputy authority, a person must fulfill three fundamental requirements (in addition to knowing God's authority and submitting to His authority).

Recognizing That All Authorities Come from God

A deputy authority must remember that all authorities come from God. God is the One who has established all authorities. If there is any authority in a man at all, that authority comes from God. There is no inherent authority in a person, and no one can appoint himself to be an authority. Our personal opinions cannot become others' law, and our own ideas, views, and proposals do not deserve others' esteem; they are no better than those who are under us. We have to remember that all authority comes from God. In fact, the only authority that is authority at all is the authority that comes from God, and only such authority can claim submission from others. We can only ask the brothers and sisters to submit to the authority in us which comes from God. A deputy authority can only be a deputy to God's authority. He cannot presume that he has any authority in himself just because he has become a deputy authority. This is a basic problem with us today. All deputy authorities must remember that they are merely God's representative authorities; they have no authority in themselves.

No matter whether we are in the world, in the church, or in God's work, we must always remember that we have absolutely no authority in ourselves. None of us have any authority in ourselves. We must remember that no one in the whole universe has authority except God. The authorities that we see today are but men executing God's authority; there are no self-made authorities. Policemen merely carry out the law. Likewise, judges merely execute the law. They can only execute the law; they cannot legislate the laws. All the officers and authorities in this world are established by God and are there only to execute the law. They execute the law on behalf of God's authority. They cannot institute any law by themselves. All authorities in the church today are likewise deputies of God's authority. The reason we have authority is simply because we are representing God's authority. There is no intrinsic element in ourselves that sets us apart from others or that gives us the right to be an authority.

A person becomes an authority because of his knowledge of God's will, God's mind, and God's thoughts. One does not become an authority based on his own ideas or opinions, but through an apprehension of God's will and desire. One cannot expect others to submit to his own will or opinion. The extent one represents authority depends on the extent of one's knowledge of God's will and thoughts. God appoints a person to be a deputy authority because such a person knows His will and His thoughts more than others, not because he has more suggestions, better ideas, or higher thoughts. Actually, this is the kind of people we are most afraid of in the church. They think that they have better ideas and opinions, and they assume to be the authority and impose themselves upon others.

Many young co-workers and saints have not learned the lessons; they do not know God's will or thoughts. This is why God has placed them under you. As the authority to them, you have the responsibility to tell them God's will and thoughts. Please remember that you have nothing in yourself that can claim submission from others. It is only when you become acquainted with God's will that you can ask others to submit to the authority in you. Every time that you have to deal with someone, you must have the assurance from God that you understand His will and that you know what God wants to do in that instance. Once you become clear about the Lord's way of dealing with the situation, you can act as the authority. Only then can you serve others with your authority. Without this you do not possess any authority to which others should submit.

No one who does not learn to submit to God's authority or who is ignorant of His will can become God's deputy authority. Suppose a man represents a company to negotiate business with others. He cannot make an offer according to his own ideas. He cannot make a promise based on his own likes, and he cannot make his own decision to sign a contract. He must first find out his manager's plan and know what his manager wants him to say and under what circumstances and conditions he can sign the contract. In the same way, if a man wants to be God's deputy authority, he must first understand God's will and His way. Only then can he execute God's authority. To be a representative authority, one must first be acquainted with the person whom he represents. He cannot have his own ideas, thoughts, or words. God's deputy authority must first know God's will. He cannot pass on an order to the brothers and sisters that God has not issued. Suppose you tell someone to do something, and suppose he has the chance to go to the Lord together with you to inquire of the matter. If God does not acknowledge what you have said to the brothers, you will be left representing only yourself, not God. This is why you have to understand God's will and execute it on God's behalf. If you do this, God will acknowledge what you do. You can have authority only when God acknowledges your decision. Anything that issues from yourself bears no authority whatsoever.

In spiritual matters, we have to learn to always climb higher and strike deeper. We must always seek for a deeper and richer knowledge of God's ways and will. We need much revelation and learning. We need to learn many things and acquire all kinds of experiences. We have to see what others have not seen and touch what others have not touched. What we do must be based on what we have learned before the Lord, and what we say must be based on what we have perceived and experienced before the Lord. If we have sufficient experience before the Lord, and if we have sufficiently learned His ways, we will have the boldness to declare that this is what we know from God, that this is what we have learned of Him, and that this is what we have experienced in Him. When we do this, we will have authority. Without

God, there is no authority. Those who have not seen anything before God have no authority before men. All authorities are based on our knowledge and learning before God. Some older ones may think that they can impose their ideas upon the younger ones. Some brothers may think that they can impose themselves upon the sisters, and some quick ones may think that they can impose themselves upon the slow ones. But such self-acts will never work. If you want to be an authority to others and want others to submit to your authority, the first thing you have to do is know authority yourself. You have to realize that you have no authority in yourself. What you should have is knowledge of God and an apprehension of His will. Only then can you be a deputy to God's authority.

Learning to Deny Ourselves

The second basic requirement of a deputy authority is to deny himself. Before one is clear about God's will, he should not open his mouth and should not exercise any authority. God's deputy authority must not only know His authority on the positive side, but must learn to deny himself on the negative side. Please remember that neither God nor the brothers and sisters treasure your opinion. I am afraid that the only one who treasures your opinion in the whole world is yourself. If you think your opinion is the best, that God treasures your opinion, and that the brothers and sisters honor your idea, you are living in a dream. Do not be so foolish as to unilaterally impose your opinion upon others. We are afraid of those with much opinion, and we are also afraid of those with many ideas, those who like to be others' counselors. We are afraid of men who are too subjective. Many people are very subjective, and they like to be counselors to others. They make proposals and plans for others in every-thing. The minute they are given the opportunity, they put forward their proposals. These ones can never be a president, a chairman, or a policeman. However, even though they may not be in certain positions, they think they know what those in such positions should do. They like to propose for others. As soon as they are given the chance, they open their mouth to express their ideas and air their opinions before others.

Even if they are not given the chance, they still try to barge in for a word or two. If they cannot find an opportunity to speak in front of others, they will try to do it behind others. Please remember that God would never appoint anyone with a great deal of opinions, proposals, and views to be His deputy authority. We would not ask a person who loves to spend money to manage our bank account, because we do not want to suffer loss. In the same way, God does not ask a person who loves to express his opinion to be His deputy authority, because He does not want to suffer loss either.

The Lord must first thoroughly break our self before we can become His deputy authority. According to my personal observation, I have never seen God choose an opinionated person to be His deputy authority. Such a one must first go through God's breaking and give up his interest in meddling in others' affairs and acting as others' counselors. God wants us to *represent* His authority, not *replace* His authority. It is true that we are like God in many ways. But He remains the sovereign One in His Godhead and position. His will belongs to Him alone; it is supreme and sovereign above everything else. He never seeks counsel from us, and He never wants us to be His counselor. This is why God's deputy authority must not be subjective. Of course, in order to conduct business, there is the need for decisions and judgments. It does not mean that God will only use those who have no ideas, opinions, or judgments in anything. It means that we must be genuinely broken, our wisdom must be destroyed, and our opinions and proposals must be crushed before God can use us. The basic problem with many people is that by nature they are active in their mind; they speak a great deal and make many proposals. They are naturally clever and like to be others' counselors. Such ones have to pray for mercy from God. They need a basic dealing and a basic breaking. This is not an empty slogan, a teaching, or a kind of imitation. A man must receive a fundamental dealing and breaking, and there must be an open wound; his own wisdom, opinion, and ideas must be crushed and broken. Such a person spontaneously will be free of his own thoughts and ideas. A man who has passed through God's chastisement is one who lives in fear before the Lord. He will no longer dare speak carelessly. He will always be afraid of making mistakes. As long as God's wound remains in a man, he will feel the pain the minute he moves, and no one will need to remind him of his wound.

If a man only knows the teaching of brokenness and is only putting on a performance by imitating others in keeping his mouth shut, his true nature will be exposed sooner or later. Some people are by nature talkative and opinionated. It is difficult to see them shut their mouth and not express their opinion. Such ones may pick up some teachings on brokenness and realize that they should not talk so much or make so many proposals. If they begin to imitate others and follow their example, their fig leaves soon will dry up (Gen. 3:7), and their underlying condition will be exposed. We cannot control ourselves with our will. If we try to control ourselves with our will, our true self will be exposed as soon as we are engaged in a heated discussion, and we will find ourselves confessing our sins to God again. We need nothing less than the killing of our self by God's light. God has to allow us to bump against the wall until our skull is cracked and our bones come apart. We must go through an experience like that of Balaam in Numbers 22:25. God needs to inflict a wound on us so that as soon as we move again, we will feel the hurt and not dare make any more proposals. When a man is wounded, there is no need for others to exhort him to walk slowly; he spontaneously will slow his pace. This is the only way that will deliver us from our self. This is why I have often said that we need wounds. Others must find open wounds in us. There is no other way to go on except through a thorough confession and dealing before God.

Those who are the deputy authorities must learn not to propose any opinion of their own or express their own ideas. They must not have an addiction for meddling in others' affairs. Some people think that they are the supreme justices; they think they know how to manage everything, whether it is things in the world, things in the church, or anything at all. They think that they know everything, and that they have an idea and a solution for everything. When others come to them, they gladly give away their advice. If others do not come to them, they still give away their advice freely like spreading the gospel. Such opinionated ones have never been disciplined; they have never gone through any severe dealings. They may have experienced some minor and superficial dealings, but their opinions, ideas, and methods still abound. They seem to be omnipotent and omniscient. Their opinions are like open merchandise in a department store. Such ones can never be an authority. Every deputy authority of God must have one basic qualification—they must not have an inclination for careless opinions or criticism. They should not even have murmuring opinions or unexpressed proposals in their heart. Only those whose self has been dealt with in such a way are qualified to be God's deputy authority.

The Need for Constant Fellowship with the Lord

Those who are God's deputy authorities should possess a third qualification—they must have a constant and intimate fellowship with the Lord. There must not only be a *communion,* but a *communication.* Some are loaded with opinions throughout the day. These ones must learn to give up their opinions. Every time one has an opinion, he has to bring it to the Lord and find out if such an opinion is of the flesh or of God. In this way God will gradually reveal His heart's desire to him. This is the basic need. The fundamental problem with many people is that they open their mouth without ever approaching God. They express their opinions loosely and speak for the Lord carelessly because they are far from God. The easier it is for a person to mention God's name, the more it proves that he is far from God. Only those who are near to God have a fear of Him, and only these ones can feel the repugnancy of wild opinions. For example, many villagers here in Kuling are lumbermen. They can freely criticize the government and the leaders of our country. But in Nanking or Chungking (capitals in China) one does not hear criticism from the people. Even though people here speak of the president freely, if he came to Kuling, everyone would address him as "Sir" or "Mr. President" in a respectful way.

No one would dare address him disrespectfully. In the same way, only those who are near to God have a fear of and respect for Him. They would not dare walk loosely or speak in the Lord's name.

We must realize that fellowship is a basic qualification for being an authority. The more we come to the Lord and draw near to Him, the more we become conscious of our mistakes. We will see that many of the actions that we previously considered as right were actually wrong. The more we know God, the more things will appear different to us. There were things which we were so sure of ten or twenty years ago. What is our view of them now? Many times you may say to yourself, "Why was I so blind? Why was I so confident and so sure that I was right?" The same thing that seemed right before may be shown to be totally wrong today. Once you have met God face to face, you will no longer be so sure in your speaking, you will no longer be so self-confident, and you will begin to be afraid of making mistakes. If the things we were so sure of in the past can be found to be wrong today, what will happen to the things that we are so sure of today? Hence, if we are persons who are in constant fellowship with the Lord, we will never open our mouths rashly. The less a person knows himself, the more he will boast about what he knows. Loose speaking is a proof that one is far from God.

The fear of the Lord is not an outward performance. Only those who constantly come near to God can fear God. However, a wild person who has no control over himself is far from God. As soon as the queen of Sheba saw Solomon, there was no more spirit in her (1 Kings 10:4-5). But today something more than Solomon is here (Matt. 12:42). When we go before the Lord, there should be "no more spirit" in us; we should not dare speak His name lightly or open our mouth rashly. We should be like a servant waiting at the door, telling God that we know nothing. May the Lord deliver us from the sickness of speaking what we do not understand and making judgments on what we do not know. Sometimes we have to take action immediately, yet we are not a person in constant fellowship with God, and we make decisions in the spur of the moment. This is a big problem in many people. No problem is more serious than that of a servant of God speaking rashly when he is unsure of God's will. It is indeed a big problem for a man to make judgments about a matter before he is even clear of anything before the Lord; such a one is never clear, yet he is ever speaking. We can be clear about God's will only when we live before Him and draw near to Him all the time.

The Lord Jesus said, "The Son can do nothing from Himself except what He sees the Father doing, for whatever that One does, these things the Son also does in like manner" (John 5:19). He also said, "I can do nothing from Myself; as I hear, I judge, and My judgment is just, because I do not seek My own will but the will of Him who sent Me" (v. 30). We have to learn to hear, to understand, and to see. All these abilities are derived from an intimate fellowship with the Lord. Only those who are living in the presence of God can listen, understand, and see. Only those who have learned the lessons can know God's will, and only as they live in God's presence can they speak to the brothers and sisters. When problems arise among the saints or in the church, these ones will know what to do. Unless a person practices this, he will be taking the name of the Lord in vain.

Please give me the liberty to say a frank word. The problem with many of God's servants today is that they are too bold, or to put it in a stronger way, they are too reckless. They have never learned to listen to God's word, and they have never seen any revelation or understood God's will, yet they have the audacity to speak for God! Let me ask you: What kind of authority do you have in speaking? Who has given you authority? What makes you different from the other brothers and sisters? If you do not have the assurance that what you speak is God's word, what authority do you hold? If I brought you and someone who has a dispute with you to the Lord, would you have the confidence to say that everything you have said was of the Lord? If God acknowledges your words, it would be all right. But if God does not acknowledge your words, what authority would you really have? You must remember that authority is deputized to you; it is not intrinsically yours. If you are not representing God's authority, what right do you have to speak or work?

All of God's deputy authorities must live before God and learn to fellowship with Him. You must be dealt with by Him, and there must be scars upon your body. When you speak to the saints or in the church, you must not insert your self into your speaking but must have the assurance that there is authority behind your words. Never be deceived to think that you have any authority in yourself. Never think that any authority has its source in you. You must forever remember that God is the only One who has the authority, and no one else. The Bible says clearly that all authority is of God.

If there is any authority in me today, such authority comes from God. I am only the channel through which authority flows. Other than this distinction, I am the same as everyone else; I am no different from the most foolish man. What sets me apart from others and gives me the authority is God, not anything in myself. Therefore, we have to learn to fear God and to fellowship with Him. This is not a light matter. We should tell the Lord, "I am no different from all the other brothers and sisters." If God has arranged for us to bear some authority and learn to be a deputy authority, we have to learn to live before Him and have constant fellowship with Him. We have to ask Him to show us His heart's desire. Only when we see something before God can we minister it to the brothers and sisters, and only then are we qualified to be a deputy authority.

Why do we use the word *communication* in discussing fellowship with God? It is because fellowship is not something that we can take care of once for all before the Lord; it requires that we live in the Lord's presence continually. Communication is a lifelong exercise. We can learn some basic lessons once for all. But living in the presence of the Lord is a continual matter. Once we move away from God, authority becomes perverted, and the flavor changes. Hence, we have to live before the Lord continually and fear Him all the time. We should always bear in mind that we should be those who have passed through God's judgment. Since God wants to use us, we must live in His presence all the time.

The above three items are the basic qualifications of a deputy authority. Authority is of God,.and we are merely His deputies. All authority belongs to God. Therefore, man cannot be subjective and must deny himself. This is why we need to live moment by moment in fellowship with Him. Since authority belongs to God, we have no authority of our own. We are merely representatives. Authority does not belong to me; therefore, I cannot be subjective. I must live in fellowship. Once fellowship is cut off, authority is gone. Those who are in authority are placed in an awkward position—they cannot quit and they cannot relax. How very different this is from human concepts. No one who truly knows God would like to be an authority. To be a deputy authority is a great matter; it is a serious thing.

NOT ESTABLISHING ONE'S OWN AUTHORITY

Since God is the One who establishes authority, there is no need for deputy authorities to try to build up their own authority. I know of a few brothers and sisters who were so foolish in the past that they thought they could direct others with their authority. They were trying to build up their own authority. This is foolish in the eyes of God. Hebrews 5:4 says, "No one takes the honor upon himself, but only as he is called by God." The same is true with authority; no one can take authority upon himself. When God grants one to be an authority, he has authority. Hence, there is no need to demand obedience from others. If others insist on being wrong, let them be wrong. If others will not obey, leave them alone. If others want to take their own way, let them take their own way. We must never argue with others. If I am not appointed by God to be the authority, why do I have to demand obedience from others? On the other hand, if I am an authority appointed by God, why do I have to worry that others will not submit to me? If there is authority with me, others are disobeying God when they disobey me. So why do I need to be concerned with others' disobedience? If authority is with me, others will be arguing with God when they argue with me. There is nothing more serious than this in the whole world. We do not need to force others to listen to us; we can give everyone the liberty to do what they want. If God backs up the authority, what more do we have to fear? Have you ever seen a king on earth backing up his ministers? No! However, if you are a deputy authority, God will sustain you, support you, and even back you up.

The more we know authority and the more open doors, revelation, and ministry we have, the more we will give others the liberty to take their own way. We must never speak one word to vindicate our own authority; rather, we should give others the full liberty. Others should come to us in as spontaneous a way as possible. If they do not want us to be their authority, or if they shy away from us, we do not have to force them to accept us. If there is authority in us, whoever desires the Lord will gladly come to us. It is a most ugly thing for anyone to speak for his authority in order to establish authority for himself. No one can establish his own authority. What one can minister to others in a locality can never be replaced by anyone else. If you have a ministry and others do not submit to you, they are the ones who will suffer the loss. God's government is a mysterious thing. Many people think that they are growing spiritually, but unless they continue in obedience, God's light will stop. They may not realize it after just one or two days, but after a while, they invariably will fall.

We have a good example in David. He was a person who never tried to establish his own authority. After Saul was rejected and David was anointed by God to be king, David still spent many years under Saul. He did not move his own hands to build up his own authority. If God has appointed you to be the authority, you must be able to pay the price to allow others to oppose you, disobey you, and rebel against you. But if you are not God's appointed authority, it would be useless to even try to build up your own authority. I do not like to hear some husbands speak to their wives, saying, "I am God's appointed authority and you must obey me," or some elders speak to saints in the church, saying, "I am God's appointed authority." If you are a deputy authority, others will spontaneously submit to you. If they do not submit, they will fall back, and if they oppose you, they will not be able to go on spiritually. Paul said that all who were in Asia had turned away from him (2 Tim. 1:15). Those who had forsaken Paul could never advance spiritually. Brothers and sisters, never try to build up your own authority. If God has appointed you to be the authority, simply accept it. If God has not appointed you to be the authority, why do you have to strive for it? All self-established authority must be eradicated from among us. We must allow God to establish every authority, and we must not try to build up any authority of our own. If God has indeed commissioned us to be the authority, others will have only two ways to take: Either they can disobey and fall or they can obey and be blessed.

WHEN A DEPUTY AUTHORITY IS TESTED

When a deputy authority is tested, he has to trust in God's government. There is no need to worry, defend, speak for oneself, or do anything at all. I dislike and abhor those who say, "I am God's appointed authority." When we set out for our work, we will find much opposition, lawlessness, and rebellion. But if we are truly a deputy authority, we do not have to build up our own authority or try to maintain it. If a man rebels, he is not rebelling against us, but against God. If he rebels, he is not offending our authority, but God's authority. We are merely here to act as the deputy authority. The One who is shamed, criticized, and opposed is God, not us. If God can endure these things, can we not endure them? Who are we? We are just the lowly ones who follow Jesus Christ of Nazareth. It is only right that we be despised. If we have not seen this, may the Lord be merciful to us. We have to realize that when others offend authority, they are not offending us, but the authority that is in us. I can speak from my own experience. If our authority is of God and others oppose and damage us, they are the ones who suffer loss; they will have no future spiritually; their revelation will stop. God's government is a most sobering matter! We must learn to not trust in ourselves. We must fear God and know what authority is. May the Lord be gracious to us!

CHAPTER THIRTEEN

THE BASIS OF GOD'S DEPUTY AUTHORITY— REVELATION

Scripture Reading: Exo. 3:1-12; Num. 12:1-15

In the Old Testament the greatest authority God appointed was Moses. We can learn many lessons from him. We will put aside for now the general and lifelong dealings that Moses went through. Instead, we will pay attention to the description of his reaction when his authority was offended, mocked, opposed, and rejected. Moses was rejected and opposed several times, and each time he reacted in the proper way.

Before Moses was appointed by God to be the authority, he killed an Egyptian who had slain one of his kinsmen. Afterwards, he exhorted two Hebrews to not argue with each other. But the two Hebrews turned around and asked him, "Who made thee a prince and a judge over us?" (Exo. 2:14). At that time Moses had not yet learned his lesson; he did not know the cross or the meaning of resurrection; he acted purely by the strength of his flesh. As a result, he could not stand the test. He had killed someone and rebuked others and appeared to be quite bold, yet within he was weak. As soon as he was tested he became afraid. He ran away to the wilderness of the Midianites in fear, and stayed there for forty years to learn his lesson (vv. 11-22). After he passed through many trials, God showed him the vision of the burning bush. The bush appeared to be burning, but it was not consumed. The fire did not consume the bush. After God showed Moses this revelation, He called him and made him the authority. It was after such a training and such a calling that he was qualified to be a leader. After he became the leader, he experienced rejection by others many times. In one instance, his brother Aaron and his sister Miriam reviled him, criticized him, and rejected him as the deputy authority. Let us see how he responded.

THE REACTION OF THE DEPUTY AUTHORITY WHEN BEING REJECTED

Not Listening to Reviling Words

According to Numbers 12:1-2, Moses married a Cushite woman, and Aaron and Miriam spoke against him for this. In this section we see the degree of spiritual loss they suffered as a result of their reviling of deputy authority, and we also see Moses' reaction as God's deputy authority. Aaron and Miriam were in effect challenging Moses: "Can it be possible that only you, Moses, who married a Cushite woman, can speak for God? Can we not do the same? You are a descendant of Shem, and you married a descendant of Ham. Can a person like you be a spokesman for God? Is it possible that we who have never married a descendant of Ham are barred from being God's mouthpiece also?" They might have argued a great deal with their sister-in-law, but the real problem was that they were touching Moses as the deputy authority. At this point verse 2 says, "And Jehovah heard it." It does not say that Moses heard it. Here we see a man who was not touched by man's word. He was a person beyond man's reviling. We see a transcendent man, a man of authority. All opposition, reviling, and rebellion were under his feet. He let God listen to the many words while he himself did not lend an ear to them.

Those who desire to be a minister of God's word, who want to speak for God, and who aspire to take the lead among the brothers and sisters should learn to have no ear for reviling words. We should let God listen to those many words; we should reserve the words for God. We should never pay attention to how others criticize or revile us. Those who find out what others say about them and then get angry, indignant, or vindictive are not qualified to be a deputy authority. Those who can be affected by revilings or who can be crushed by such words cannot be a deputy authority. Moses was a person untouched by reviling words.

Not Vindicating

When Moses was reviled, he did not vindicate himself. All vindication, justification, and reaction should come from God, not from man. Those who seek to vindicate themselves do not know God. No one who has walked on this earth has had more authority than Christ. But when the Lord was on earth, He never vindicated Himself. He is the only person who never vindicated Himself. Authority and vindication are incompatible. Whenever we try to vindicate ourselves before someone, it means that the person is our judge. Whenever we vindicate ourselves before those who criticize us, we are telling them that they are higher than us. A vindicating person is a person who is under the judgment of others. Those who vindicate themselves have no authority whatsoever. Whenever a person vindicates himself, he loses his authority. God may have committed His authority to us, but if we vindicate ourselves before men, we have lost our authority because we are begging them to be our judge.

Paul was a deputy authority to the Corinthians, yet he said, "It is a very small thing that I should be examined by you or by man's day; rather I do not even examine myself" (1 Cor. 4:3). Vindication can only come from God. We should pass on all reviling and critical words to the Lord. When man's revilings become too much, God will take action. But if we vindicate ourselves to anyone, we are in effect making him our judge. If we seek understanding from anyone, we are falling under that person's feet. Hence, we must never vindicate ourselves and must never seek understanding from anyone.

Full of Meekness

In Numbers 12:2 God heard the reviling words, and He took action in verse 4. But there is a parenthetical word in verse 3: "Now the man Moses was very meek, more than all the men who were on the face of the earth." This is what we find in a God-appointed deputy authority. Why did Moses not hear their reviling words? Perhaps Moses thought that he was indeed wrong and did not want to argue with them. God cannot make a stubborn person His authority. He cannot appoint a belligerent man to be His deputy authority. The authorities God establishes in the church are meek and inconspicuous. God does not appoint persons of great charisma to be His authority; He appoints those who are not only meek in a general way, but meek to the extent that their meekness exceeds that of all the men who are on the face of the earth. In other words, they are as meek as God is.

A deputy authority can never build up his own authority. The more a person tries to build up his own authority, the less he is qualified to be the authority. Authority is from God; hence, vindication must also be from God. We pray that we do not meet too many hardened persons. Do not get the wrong idea that a hard and capable person would make a good deputy authority. We should be very clear that only a person like Paul, whose bodily presence was weak, can be the authority. The Lord said that His kingdom was not of this world, and therefore His attendants did not need to struggle (John 18:36). God's kingdom is not established through struggling. All authority earned through struggling is not authority from God.

Please remember that Moses was meek above all the men who were on the face of the earth. This is why he could be a deputy authority. If I ask you to list the traits of a deputy authority, I believe that nine out of ten of you would list such things as good and proper appearance, strong charisma, great power, or an imposing image. The human thought is that an authority should be capable, imposing, powerful, assertive, and eloquent. But such traits do not represent authority; rather, they represent the flesh. No other God-appointed authority in the Old Testament was as great as Moses, yet He was a most meek person. When he was in Egypt, he was quite fierce. He killed an Egyptian and rebuked two Hebrews. He dealt with others with his fleshly hands, but God did not use him as His authority then. Only after he had passed through God's testing and dealing, becoming so meek that his meekness was above all the men who were on the face of the earth, did he become an authority. The less a person truly resembles an authority, the more he feels that he is an authority. The more a person thinks that he is an authority, the less it is likely that he is an authority.

REVELATION BEING THE BASIS OF AUTHORITY

Numbers 12:4 says, "And suddenly Jehovah said to Moses and to Aaron and Miriam, Come out, you three, to the tent of meeting." Here the Lord spoke suddenly. *Suddenly* means something unexpected. Aaron and Miriam might have criticized Moses many times, but the Lord suddenly called them to the tent of meeting. Many people criticize easily and act against authority lightly. They speak against others loosely because they are living in their own tent; they are far away from the tent of meeting. When a man is in his own tent, it is easy for him to criticize. But once he enters the tent of meeting, everything becomes clear to him. All three came before the tent of meeting, and Jehovah said to Aaron and Miriam, "Hear My words" (v. 6a). They first questioned if it was fair that God only spoke to Moses, and now God summoned them to hear His words too. This shows that they had never learned to hear God's word and had never known what it was like for God to speak. On that day Jehovah spoke to them for the first time. Indeed, God was speaking, but He spoke words of rebuke, not words of revelation. It was not for the manifestation of God's glory, but for the judgment of their actions. He said, "Hear My words." It was as if He were saying, "I did not say anything in the past, but let Me say something now." This word may also mean, "You have been speaking for so long and so often. Now give Me a chance to speak. You who are so good at speaking, listen to Me today." A talkative person cannot hear God's word; only a meek person can hear His word. Moses was meek, not talkative. He could turn any way the Lord wanted him to turn; he could go forward or backward. But Aaron and Miriam were stubborn.

After this God said, "If there is a prophet among you..." (v. 6b), as if He did not know that there was a prophet among them. It sounded as if God had forgotten something. But God said that even if there were a prophet, God would at most speak to him in a vision or in a dream (v. 6c). But with

Moses, God spoke mouth to mouth, clearly, and not in obscure words (v. 8). This was God's vindication. God's speaking to Moses came in the way of revelations and light; they were very clear. Moses did not vindicate himself. It was God who vindicated him. It is true that everyone who is sent in the name of the Lord to speak to God's children has some degree of authority. But I do hope that you will not try to establish your own authority. I hope that you will not vindicate yourselves. Revelation was granted to Moses alone, not to Aaron or Miriam. Whoever speaks with God face to face is God's appointed authority. The establishment of authority is based upon God's choice; it is God's business, and man cannot interfere in any way. Neither is the annulling of authority achieved through man's reviling. God could appoint Moses, and He could also annul Moses. But whether it was appointment or annulling, it was God's business; man had no right to question it. Man could not annul Moses' authority with reviling words. A man's worth before the Lord is not based on others' evaluation of him nor his own evaluation of himself. A man's worth before the Lord is based on revelation. Revelation is the standard of God's measure and valuation. The establishment of authority is based on God's revelation, and God evaluates a person based on revelation. As soon as a person is set aside by the Lord, he loses his revelation, and God no longer speaks to him. God said that Moses was His servant and that He spoke with him mouth to mouth. If God grants us revelation, everything will be fine. If He does not grant us revelation, nothing will work. Aaron and Miriam complained, and God seemed to ask, "How much revelation do you have? All My revelation is with Moses."

In order to learn to be the authority, we have to consider what we are before the Lord. When we set out for our work, the test is not in Aaron's or Miriam's measuring, but in God's measuring. If God grants us revelation, and we have a clear word from Him and face-to-face fellowship with Him, no one can annul us. But if the way upward is not clear and heaven is not open to us, nothing will avail even if all the doors on earth are open to us. If heaven is open to us, we will have God's vindication. We will have the proof of being a son of

God, that is, the proof of sonship. When the Lord was baptized, heaven opened (Matt. 3:16). Baptism is a symbol of death. When the Lord was crucified on the cross, He entered death and was placed in the tomb. When darkness is at its worst, when pain reaches its height, and when all doors are shut, heaven opens. Revelation is the basis of authority. We must learn to not fight for ourselves or speak for ourselves. We should not be like Aaron or Miriam, clamoring for authority. If after you leave here you fight for authority, it will prove that you are in the flesh and in darkness. It will also prove that you have not seen anything here on the mountain.

GOD'S SERVANT

In Numbers 12:7, God said, "My servant Moses...is faithful in all My house." This word is later quoted in the New Testament book of Hebrews. Hebrews shows us that Moses, as a type of Christ the Son of God, was faithful in all God's house (3:2). God seemed to be hinting at Aaron and Miriam, saying, "Moses might not have been altogether faithful in your house when he married a Cushite woman. But he serves My people and is faithful in all My house. You spoke against him because his wife may not have been a good sister-in-law in your house, but he is My servant. Why are you not afraid when you speak against My servant Moses?"

God called Moses His servant. For me to be God's servant means that I belong to God. I am God's inheritance, and I have been sold to God. If I ever become lost, it will be God's loss, not my loss. Those who own servants lose their property when they lose their servants. Moses was God's servant, which means that he was God's property, and when anyone spoke against His servant, God surely had to step forward to speak for him. We do not have to defend ourselves, and there is no need for us to build up our own authority. This is God's business. I am His servant, and when I am spoken against, God will step forward. If God does not step forward, what use would there be for me to step forward myself? Why is there the need to build up my own authority at all? If God is the One who appoints me to be the authority, I should not do anything to establish myself; I should only allow revelation to vindicate me. If I find revelation and supply in others also, it proves that God has not vindicated me. But if God has established me, He will seal up others as a vindication for me. If you are a deputy authority and others dispute this, they are disputing God. If they have any life in them at all, they will experience a closed heaven, and they will bow to you and acknowledge your authority.

I hope that no one would stand up to claim that he is the authority. You should allow time and revelation to vindicate you. Revelation is the best vindication. Suppose you say that God has chosen you and that you have revelation and authority. If others oppose and rebel against you, and if they go to God and also receive revelation, it means that God has not vindicated you or backed you up. In that case it would be useless to speak for yourself. If you are faithful in all of God's house and put everything you have into His house, and if you find Him sealing up others, it means that He has appointed you to be His authority. Authority is something in God's hand; it does not depend on you. The greatest problem today is man's self. If you understand what is God's authority and God's way, you will realize what I have been saying repeatedly, that is, when others argue with you, they are arguing with God, because you are God's possession. As soon as others touch you, God seals up their heaven, and they have no choice but to turn and repent, acknowledging you as God's authority. Hence, there is no need to build up your own authority. Everything depends on God's vindication. If God seals up others, it means that He has appointed you to be the authority.

NO PERSONAL FEELINGS

At the end of verse 8 God said, "Why then were you not afraid to speak against My servant, against Moses?" God knows that there are some things to be fearful of. God is God; He knows what love is, what light is, what glory is, and what holiness is. God even knows what fear is because He feared for Aaron and Miriam. He asked, "Why then were you not afraid to speak against My servant, against Moses?" God is afraid of nothing, but He told Aaron and Miriam that speaking against Moses was a fearful thing. To God this was a matter to be feared. Unless they were altogether in darkness, ignorance, and senselessness, they should have been afraid. At this point God stopped. He did not execute His judgment yet, but He departed, His anger burning against them (v. 9).

God expends much energy to maintain His authority. Let me solemnly repeat this: God maintains His own authority; He does not maintain Moses' authority. We can say respectfully that when God's servant commits a mistake, it is God's business alone. God did not say, "You have spoken against Moses;" rather, He said that they had spoken against "My servant, against Moses." It so happened that in this case, God's servant was Moses. But if it had been someone else, it would have been the same; it would have been "My servant," plus the name of the servant. God was here maintaining His own authority; He was not maintaining Moses' authority. God would not allow anyone to infringe on His authority. As soon as man rebels against His authority, He turns away in wrath.

As soon as God left, the cloud was removed from over the tent (v. 10). The cloud represents God's presence. For the cloud to leave means that God's presence was removed. Typically, when the cloud moved on, God moved on, and the tabernacle moved on as well. But when the cloud moved this time, Miriam became leprous. Typically, the moving of the cloud marked the start of the Israelites' journey. But on that day, they could not journey on, because rebellion had broken out. When Aaron saw this he was afraid, because he had partaken of this rebellion. Since Miriam had taken the lead in this rebellion, she was the one who became leprous.

Moses did not open his mouth. As long as the tabernacle did not communicate any revelation, Moses did not open his mouth. He had learned his lesson. Although he was eloquent, he kept his mouth shut and did not open it until Aaron pleaded for forgiveness. Those whose hearts and mouths are not bridled are not qualified to be the authority. Those who have God's authority surely have it in their heart as well as their mouth. When Aaron pleaded with Moses, he cried to Jehovah. Before that time, Moses was a bystander. There was no murmuring in him. There was no rebuke or criticism in him. When Aaron pleaded with him, he prayed. This is the cross. Here we find that Moses was a person who did not have any personal feeling. When he saw Miriam becoming leprous and Aaron pleading out of fear, he immediately cried to God. He did not say coldly, "All right, as a favor to you I will perhaps try to plead with God for you." No! Moses cried to God immediately. He did not have any feeling of his own. He had no thought of justification or punishment. When God's purpose was fulfilled, he forgave immediately. Authority is for executing God's command; it is not for uplifting oneself. A deputy authority should bring the presence of God to God's children, not the presence of himself. We are here to bring others under God's authority, not our authority. It is a small thing for us to be rejected. In verse 13 Moses prayed, "Heal her, O God, I beg You." Here was a man who was truly qualified to be an authority because he had no feeling of his own. May the Lord deliver us from our personal feelings. Once a man is entangled with his personal feelings, God's business suffers and He becomes restricted.

Moses did not take pleasure in Aaron and Miriam's suffering. On the contrary, he asked God for mercy and prayed for Miriam's healing. Had Moses not received mercy and had he been ignorant of God's grace, he would have said to Aaron, "Since you have said that God should speak to you also, why don't you pray to God yourself?" Or he could have said to God, "If You do not vindicate me, I will quit." It seems that God was giving Moses a chance to vindicate himself. Moses did not ask for such a chance; it came by itself. Moses could have said: "Had God been silent, I could not have done anything. But now that God has done something, I can take this opportunity to vindicate myself." But he did not take the opportunity to vindicate or revenge. He could have said to God, "My brother and sister are criticizing me. If You do not do anything for me, I will quit." It is easy for a man to seize the moment of God's vindication to vindicate himself and take revenge. But Moses did not justify himself, nor did he take advantage of God's vindication. He did not have any feeling of his own; he was a person who was not living in his self. Such criticism seemed very insignificant to him. Moses' flesh had been completely dealt with. He did not revenge. On the contrary, he prayed for God to heal Miriam. This is like Christ praying on the cross for His persecutors (Luke 23:34). Some people think that it is an easy thing to be God's deputy authority. But it is not an easy thing. One has to empty himself completely before he can be a deputy authority.

Moses was indeed a true representative of the Son of God. He was able to act as God's deputy authority because he truly represented God. He was not touched by the flesh, and he did not protect himself or vindicate himself. He did not take revenge on his attackers. This is why God's authority could flow through him unhindered. We can say that he truly was a man who had met God's authority. He was not touched by the flesh, the carnal man, or the self at all. As such, he was qualified to be God's deputy authority.

Chapter Fourteen

THE CHARACTER OF GOD'S DEPUTY AUTHORITY—GRACIOUS TO OTHERS

Scripture Reading: Num. 16

HOW MOSES DEALT WITH REBELLION

No rebellion among the children of Israel was as great as the one recorded in Numbers 16. Korah of the tribe of Levi took the lead, joining himself with Dathan and Abiram of the tribe of Reuben. In addition, 250 of the leaders of the assembly joined them. They gathered themselves together and spoke strong words against Moses and Aaron. This was a great rebellion. The reviling in Numbers 12 was confined to Aaron and Miriam, and was merely a murmuring behind the back. But the rebellion in chapter sixteen was corporate, and it was directly against Moses and Aaron. The rebels said, "You have gone too far!...Why then do you exalt yourselves above the congregation of Jehovah?" (v. 3). Their charges were serious and severe. We should pay attention to (1) the condition of Moses, that is, his attitude, and (2) the way he dealt with the situation, that is, his answer to them.

First Reaction—Falling on His Face

Verse 4 says that Moses' first reaction was to fall on his face. This is the proper attitude of God's servant. All of the rebellious ones were standing when they spoke; only Moses fell down on his face. Here we see a man who had touched authority. He was indeed meek; he did not have any feeling of his own. He did not vindicate himself or argue. The first thing he did was fall on his face. In verses 5 through 7 he seemed to be saying, "Jehovah will make known who is His, who is holy, and whom He will choose, and He will cause him to come near to Him. There is no need for us to argue. In the morning we will all know. I dare not say anything for myself. He will show us clearly who is His. If it turns out to be you, that is fine. If it turns out to be me, that is also fine. Let God decide. We do not have to decide anything. Tomorrow we will all come before the Lord and be tested by the censers. Let the Lord decide who is the one; we do not have to fight for it. God will choose who is His. Let us come to God and be open to His speaking." Moses spoke these words meekly while he was falling on his face. However, the last few sentences were quite strong and serious: "You have gone too far, sons of Levi!" (v. 7). This was a sighing of grief from an elderly man who knew God. The Israelites had been wandering in the wilderness for a long time, and they were still not in Canaan yet. Moses was still hoping that they could go into Canaan; he was still hoping that he could recover them.

Exhortation and Recovery

Verses 8 through 11 were Moses' words of exhortation to Korah; he was trying to recover Korah. He had to deal with their accusation, which had to wait for the result of the next day. In the meantime, he was aware of the seriousness of this matter, and he was worried about them. It was not enough for him to sigh and worry; he felt that he had to exhort them as well. He seemed to say to Korah, "It is not a small thing for the sons of Levi to be chosen by God to do the service of the tabernacle of Jehovah. You should be content with this. Why do you still want to be the priests? When you do this, you do not oppose me; you oppose the Lord." Moses was a magnanimous man, and he was confident of the things he was doing. He knew the seriousness of this matter and he was worried about the sons of Korah. This is why he exhorted them. His exhortation was not a sign of arrogance, but of humility. Others were attacking him and giving him a hard time. But no matter how wrong they were, he could still exhort them. This is a sign of a truly meek person. If we allow others to continue in their mistakes, it means that our hearts are hardened and that we have no

intention to recover them. Refusal to exhort is a sign of a
lack of humility; it shows that one is proud. When Moses was
rebuked, he turned around to exhort his opposers and openly
deal with them. He even gave them a night to think about
it, hoping that they would repent.

In dealing with the rebellious ones, Moses took care of
them separately. First he dealt with Korah the Levite and
then with Dathan and Abiram. In verse 12 he sent for Dathan
and Abiram to come, but they would not come, indicating that
they wanted to break away. Here we see that even when a
deputy authority is rejected, he will not want the opposing
ones to break away. Instead, he will try to recover the lost
ones. Dathan and Abiram said, "You have brought us up out
of a land flowing with milk and honey" (v. 13). This statement
turned things around; it was exactly the opposite of the truth.
They forgot that they were making bricks in Egypt. There
was no milk or honey; there was not even straw to make the
bricks. This is like bringing a young man to the Lord who
then turns around and accuses you of bringing him to hell.
It is also like the ten spies who clearly saw the riches of
Canaan and yet would not enter, but murmured against Moses
instead. Nothing more could be done except judgment when
Dathan and Abiram's rebellion reached its peak. Moses tried
his best to recover them, but they declared twice that they
would not go up. After all this, Moses gave up his hope,
became angry, and went to Jehovah to settle the matter (v. 15).
Then he told Korah, "You and all your company shall be
present before Jehovah, you and they and Aaron, tomorrow.
And let every one of you take his censer, and put incense
upon it, and every one of you bring before Jehovah his censer,
two hundred and fifty censers; you also, and Aaron, each his
censer" (vv. 16-17). Korah's company then came before the
tent of meeting, reviling Moses and Aaron again. At this point
the glory of Jehovah appeared to the whole assembly.

God stepped forward to judge. Korah was the chief
instigator, and the assembly followed. God was prepared to
destroy not only the chief instigator but all of the assembly
as well (v. 21). But Moses fell down before the Lord again.
The first time Moses fell on his face before his brothers. The

second time he fell before the Lord. He prayed for the whole
assembly and interceded for their safety. God answered his
prayer and ordered the assembly to depart from the tents of
the wicked ones (vv. 22-24). Moses rose and went to Dathan
and Abiram. (They were of the tribe of Reuben and lived in
a separate place.) Since they would not come to Moses, he
went to them. He ordered the assembly to depart from them,
and God executed His judgment upon Korah, Dathan, and
Abiram (vv. 25-33).

Not Having a Spirit of Judgment

While God was about to execute His judgment, Moses said,
"In this shall you know that Jehovah has sent me to do all
these works, and that it has not been of my own mind" (v. 28).
Moses was a meek person. He explained why he had to do
this. It was God who ordered him to do it. According to his
own feeling, he would not judge anyone who rebelled against
him. He did it because God wanted to do it. Moses continued
to show himself to be a servant of God. He did not say that
they had offended him. He only said that they had offended
the Lord. We have to learn to touch the spirit of such a
person. There was no feeling of judgment in Moses at all. He
was a servant of God, and he only wanted to be obedient to
God. He had no feeling of his own. The only feeling he had
was that the assembly had offended God, the One who
had sent him. Following this, he told them that God had sent
him and that there would be evidence as proof of this. We
must realize that Moses could not fail here. Had Moses failed,
the Israelites' exodus out of Egypt would have been a failure.
Moses was sent by God to lead the Israelites out of Egypt,
just as Christ was sent by God to impart eternal life to men.
God had to establish Moses. The result of His judgment was
the destruction of three families and the consuming of
the 250 leaders by fire. God executed a large-scale judgment
to establish His deputy authority. The way of the rebellious
ones is the way to Hades; rebellion and death go hand in
hand. Authority is established by God, and when a man
offends God's authority, he is despising God. Here we see how
Moses acted as a deputy authority. He did not pass his own

sentence or make his own proposals, and he did not have a spirit of judgment within him.

Intercession and Propitiation

When all the Israelites saw that the earth opened its mouth, they were afraid and fled away (v. 34). But they were afraid of the judgment; they were not afraid of God. They still did not know Moses, and their hearts were not yet turned. Therefore, their fear did not do them any good. They thought it over for a night, and the next day they rebelled again. All the assembly of the sons of Israel murmured against Moses and Aaron, saying, "You have killed the people of Jehovah" (v. 41). Indeed, if a man has not touched God's grace, one cannot expect any change in him. God wanted to step forward and destroy the whole assembly immediately. Here we see how a deputy authority should react to opposition. Actually, Moses could have been very angry with the attack of the whole assembly of Israel. It was God's doing. Why did the Israelites have to blame him? They did not confront God but turned and sharply dealt with the deputy authority. Verses 42 through 45 tell us that God's reaction was faster than that of Moses or Aaron. The glory of the Lord appeared suddenly, and a cloud covered the tent of meeting. God was about to judge the whole assembly. He told Moses and Aaron to rise from the midst of the assembly. This order seemed to be saying to Moses and Aaron, "Your prayer yesterday was wrong, yet I answered it. Today I am going to destroy the whole assembly. What would you say?" God is never wrong, yet He is full of mercy. He answered the prayer the day before. Yet on this day, He would not tolerate their rebellion any longer.

For this, Moses and Aaron fell on their faces for the third time. Moses' spiritual sense was keen. He knew that prayer alone would not solve the problem this time. The sin the day before was still somewhat hidden, but the sin this day was clearly an open one. He told Aaron to come to him immediately, and he took Aaron's censer to the assembly and made propitiation for them (vv. 45-47). Moses was truly qualified to be a deputy authority. He knew the tragic end that the Israelites were going to face, and he realized that their loss would be God's loss. He pleaded for God's forgiving grace; his heart was full of compassion and mercy. This is the heart of one who knows God. Moses was not a priest; he could not offer up any sacrifice. But he knew that the situation was critical and there was no time to plead with God. He ordered Aaron to offer a sacrifice and to make propitiation for the people immediately. This is intercession plus propitiation. By then a plague had broken out. Aaron ran into the midst of the assembly and stood between the dead and the living, and the plague was stopped. Fourteen thousand seven hundred died by the plague (vv. 48-49). Had Moses and Aaron reacted more slowly, more would have died.

Here we see the kind of person Moses was and how he acted as God's deputy authority. His intention was for propitiation. His heart for propitiation was as gracious as that of the Lord. Moses' heart was for propitiation and forgiveness. He had no pleasure in judgment. The kind of person who can serve as God's deputy authority is one who represents God on the one hand and cares for and bears God's children upon his shoulders on the other hand. God's deputy authority must care for God's people. He must bear not only the obedient ones on his shoulders but also the rebellious ones. If he cares only for himself, minding how others treat him, and if he constantly complains that he cannot stand this one or that one, he is not qualified to be a deputy authority. When God looks for deputy authority, He considers not only a person's individual submission to Him but his reaction to others' opposition in his service as a deputy authority. A person's reaction to others' rebellion and opposition exposes the kind of person he is. Many people care only for their own faces. They care very much about criticisms, words, misunderstandings, and oppositions. Their own mind is occupied with themselves. They consider themselves to be the most important persons. These ones can never be God's deputy authority.

THE CHARACTER OF THE DEPUTY AUTHORITY—
GRACIOUS TO OTHERS

When you set out for your work this time, you have to learn from Moses. He was faithful in all of God's house. He was not faithful to himself. If he had allowed God's house to suffer loss, his flesh might have enjoyed some ease and comfort. But if he had done this, he would not have been faithful. We can be rejected and despised. We must still bear the affairs of God's children on our shoulders, and we must not allow God's house to suffer loss. Here we see a beautiful picture of how Moses was faithful in all of God's house. While Aaron was offering sacrifices for the children of Israel, Moses was prostrating and praying to God. He did not know what God was going to do. He let Aaron offer sacrifices and make propitiation for the people of Israel. Although the people rebelled against Moses, he turned around to bear their sins upon his shoulders. He took up their case. While they were opposing and rejecting him, he was interceding for them. Moses was the offended party, yet he was the one who pleaded for forgiveness. He was reviled, yet he was the one to intercede before God. Here we see the kind of person who can be God's deputy authority. A deputy authority must not act according to his own feeling, and he must not care for himself or be a self-centered person.

If we want to be God's deputy authority, we must learn to bear all of God's children upon our shoulders. May the Lord make us gracious persons, those who can tolerate all of God's children and who can bear His children upon our shoulders. If we only care for our own feeling, we will not have the capacity to bear the burdens of God's children. We must confess our sins. We are too narrow and too hard. We are not like Moses. God has grace in Himself, but He does not want to dispense grace directly. He wants His servants to seek after His grace inwardly while they are carrying out His righteousness outwardly. God's work is righteous outwardly, but His heart is full of grace. He wants all His servants, that is, those who are His deputy authorities, to have His heart and be full of grace as well. God wants us to be gracious to others. We should ask for more grace inwardly. This is pleasing to God. Why are there so many narrow-minded and self-caring ones? Many people cannot take any offense at all. But if God can take offenses, we should also be able to take offenses.

If we will truly bear the burden of the church and the children of God, and if we will learn to prostrate ourselves before the Lord, God will find His deputy authority on earth today. The more we dispense grace, the more we are qualified to be God's deputy authority. Being gracious to others is one characteristic of a deputy authority. Those who deal righteously with others are not qualified to be a deputy authority. We have to spend all our time in prayer for this before we can learn this lesson well. We have to learn to bless when we are reviled, to intercede for others when we are rejected, and to plead for forgiveness when we are offended. God's deputy authorities are gracious ones. All those who are for righteousness alone have need of God's mercy. We should allow only God to execute His righteousness in all things, while we ourselves should be gracious to all men. This is the character of an authority of God.

CHAPTER FIFTEEN

THE BASIS OF GOD'S DEPUTY AUTHORITY— RESURRECTION

Scripture Reading: Num. 17

The purpose of Numbers 17 is to show us the way God dealt with Israel's rebellion. In chapter sixteen there was an unprecedented rebellion, but chapter seventeen speaks of the termination of the rebellion; it shows the way to turn away from rebellion and death. What did God do? He vindicated to everyone that deputy authority is according to His appointment. He showed the Israelites His basis and reason for appointing authority. Such a basis is indispensable to every God-appointed authority. If a man is short in regard to this basis, he cannot be a deputy authority.

RESURRECTION BEING THE BASIS FOR GOD'S AUTHORITY

God commanded the twelve leaders to take twelve rods according to the twelve tribes of Israel, and put them in the tent of meeting before the ark. Then He said, "And the rod of the man whom I choose shall bud" (v. 5). A rod is a piece of wood. It is a branch that has been stripped of its leaves and roots. It once was living but now has become dead. It once derived its sap from the tree, being able to blossom and bear fruit, but now has become dead. All twelve rods were leafless, rootless, dry, and dead. Whichever one budded was the one that was chosen by God. Here we see that resurrection is the basis of God's selection. It is also the basis of authority.

Chapter sixteen speaks of man's rebellion against God's deputy authority and how man opposed God's appointed authority. Chapter seventeen speaks of God's vindication of His appointed authority. The basis of God's vindication of

His appointed authority is resurrection. By resurrection He stopped man's murmuring. Man, of course, has no right to question God in the first place, but God condescended Himself to tell man the reason and basis for His appointment of authority. The basis for His appointment of authority is resurrection. This shut the mouth of the Israelites.

Both Aaron and the Israelites were descendants of Adam and both were fleshly. By nature and according to their natural disposition, they were both sons of wrath; there was no difference between them. All twelve rods were the same. They were all leafless and rootless rods, dead and lifeless. This shows us that the basis of service is something apart from our natural life. It is the resurrection life we receive from God that gives us authority. Authority has nothing to do with man but with the resurrection that is manifested through man. Aaron was no different than all the other persons. His distinction was in God's choosing and the resurrection life which God granted him. From this we see that the basis of authority is resurrection.

THE BUDDING OF THE ROD
BEING A HUMBLING EXPERIENCE

The twelve rods spent a night before the ark. God caused Aaron's rod to bud, blossom, and bear ripe almonds. Here was a dead rod, yet God put the power of life into it. Moses took all the rods that were set before the ark and showed them to the Israelites. What did it mean for Aaron's rod to bud? First, a budding rod humbles the owner of the rod. Second, it shuts up the mouth of the owners of the other rods. What would our reaction be if we took a dry rod like that of Aaron's, which was dead and had no hope of budding, and found to our surprise that it had budded, blossomed, and borne fruit the next day? We would confess to God in tears that this was His doing. It would have nothing to do with us. It would be His glory, not our glory. Spontaneously, we would be humbled before God. This is what Paul meant when he said, "We have this treasure in earthen vessels that the excellency of the power may be of God and not out of us" (2 Cor. 4:7). Only foolish ones would try to be proud. A person who has received grace from God will surely fall down before Him, saying, "This is God's doing. I have nothing to boast of. Everything depends on God's mercy, not on man's willing or running. There is nothing that I have which has not been received. Everything that I have comes from God's selection."

Here we see that the basis of authority does not depend on man; it has nothing to do with man. When Aaron served the Lord again with his authority, he would say to the Lord, "My rod was as dead as others' rods. I can serve while they cannot serve. I have spiritual authority and they do not. But this has nothing to do with my rod. My rod was just as dry as theirs. None of our rods count; they are not the issue. They are not the reason. The only reason is God's mercy. It is God who has chosen me." From that time on, he could no longer serve by his rod, but by the budding of his rod.

THE MARK OF MINISTRY—RESURRECTION

A rod signifies human position, while budding signifies the resurrection life. As far as position is concerned, the twelve leaders of the twelve tribes occupied a position of leadership. Aaron represented the tribe of Levi and was no different than the others in his representation of his own tribe. Aaron could not serve God based on his position, because his position was the same as all the others. In fact, this was why the other tribes objected to his leadership. But what did God do? He ordered that twelve rods be placed in the tent of meeting before the ark for a night. The rod of the one whom God had chosen would bud. This is resurrection. Resurrection is the mark that God recognizes. He only recognizes those who have passed through death and resurrection as His servants. Hence, the mark of ministry is resurrection. A man cannot base his service to God on his position. He must base it on God's selection. After God caused Aaron's rod to bud, blossom, and bear fruit, the tribes saw it, and they had nothing more to say.

Authority is not something that one can fight for. It is something established by God. It has nothing to do with our position of leadership. Whether or not we are an authority depends on whether we have passed through death and resurrection. There is nothing in ourselves that sets us apart as a spiritual authority. Everything depends on grace, selection, and resurrection. A man has to degrade to a great depth of darkness and blindness before he can be proud. According to ourselves, no rod will bud even if it is left to itself for a lifetime. The problem today is that it is hard to find a person who will bow down and confess that he is the same as everyone else.

ONLY THE FOOLISH ONES BEING PROUD

When the Lord Jesus went into Jerusalem on a colt, the people cried, "Hosanna! Blessed is He who comes in the name of the Lord!" (Mark 11:9). When the colt heard the people shouting "Hosanna" and saw them spreading branches before the Lord, it could have turned around and asked the Lord, "Are they shouting to You or to me?" It could even have turned to its own mother and said, "I am better than you are after all." If the colt had done this, it would not have known the One who was riding on it. Many servants of God are often this foolish. The colt was no different than other colts. The difference was the Lord who was on the colt. It was not the colt who was being praised, but the Lord who was on the colt. When others cry "Hosanna," they are not crying to you. The branches and garments on the ground are not laid for you. Only a foolish person would say that he is better than others.

When Aaron saw his rod budding, would he not be the first one to be taken by surprise, and would he not bow down in tears and worship the Lord, saying, "Why has my rod budded? Is not my rod the same as the rods of all the others? Why is such great glory and power bestowed upon me? By itself, my rod would never bud." That which is of the flesh will always be the flesh. Aaron was the same as all the other people of God. After this experience, others could still be deceived, but not Aaron. He should have realized that all spiritual authority is from God. Today we need to realize also that there is no ground whatsoever for us to be proud. We have mercy because God is willing to grant us mercy. We are not sufficient in ourselves to undertake this ministry; our sufficiency is from God (2 Cor. 3:5). It is a strange thing that a man can claim to live before the Lord and yet not be humbled. What extreme self-confidence and foolishness would the colt have had if it assumed on that day that the praises were directed towards it! The day will come when we will realize how shameful this is. Even if we crave for glory, our glory lies in the future, not in the present.

All young brothers and sisters have to learn humility. You have to realize that it is not you who is able to go on. Do not think that just because you have learned some spiritual lessons, you are different from others. Everything depends on God's grace, and everything is from God. We can do nothing in ourselves. Aaron knew that God caused the rod to bud; it was the work of supernatural power. Through the budding God spoke to the Israelites, and He also spoke to Aaron. From that day on, Aaron knew that service was based on budding, not on oneself. If we want to serve the Lord today, we must also realize that our service is based on resurrection, and resurrection is based on God, not on us.

WHAT IS RESURRECTION?

Now my question is: What is resurrection? Resurrection is everything that is not out of our natural life, not out of ourselves, and not based on our ability. Resurrection speaks of the things that are beyond us, which we cannot do in ourselves. Any rod can be engraved with flowers or painted with colors, but no one can make it bud. We have never heard of a rod which can still bud and blossom after being used for decades. This is God's work. No woman in the world has ever given birth after her womb has been closed, but Sarah bore Isaac (Rom. 4:19). This was God's doing. Hence, Sarah typifies resurrection. What is resurrection? Resurrection means that one cannot do anything by himself, that he can only do it through God. It means that it is not by oneself, but by God. Resurrection means that one ignores what he is and trusts only in what God is. It matters little whether or not you are smarter than others or more eloquent than others. If you have any spirituality, this spirituality is not based on yourself, but on God's work in you. Suppose Aaron had been foolish enough to say to others, "My rod is different from your rod.

My rod is smoother, brighter, and straighter. This is why it budded." How foolish and silly that would have been! If we think for a moment that we are different from others, that is the most foolish thought. Even if there is something different in us, it is the result of God's work. Resurrection means that everything is out of God.

The name *Isaac* means "laughter." Why did Abraham call his son "laughter"? He called him Isaac for two reasons. First, God promised Abraham that Sarah would give birth to a son. When Sarah heard, she laughed. It was natural for her to laugh. When she looked at herself, she could not help but laugh. Her time of childbearing was past, and her womb was closed. How could she ever bear a child? She thought that this was impossible. Therefore, when God told Abraham that she would have a child, she laughed. Second, when Sarah brought forth a son a year later, she was indeed laughing for joy. Hence, God called the child's name *Isaac* (Gen. 18:10-15; 21:1-3, 6-7), which means "laughter." The first time she laughed because of the impossibility of the promise. The second time she laughed because she discovered to her surprise that it was possible. If a man has never experienced the first laughing, he can never experience the second laughing. If a man has never realized his own inability, he can never experience God's ability. Sarah knew herself; she had full knowledge of herself. She knew that she could not make it. But as soon as she looked to God's work, she was able to laugh. What is resurrection? Resurrection means that God has given us something that we did not have in ourselves. The Bible testifies again and again that man cannot make it by himself. But many people think that they can make it. In the matter of service, if some would truly laugh at themselves, saying, "I cannot make it," they would find themselves laughing again, saying, "I did not make it. I have seen through myself. The Lord has made it for me." If there is any manifestation of authority in us, we should say to the Lord, "You are the One who has done it. It is none of my business." Resurrection means that you cannot make it and that God is the One who has done everything.

RESURRECTION BEING
THE ETERNAL PRINCIPLE OF SERVICE

The principle to every service lies in the budding rod. God returned all the eleven rods to the leaders, but kept Aaron's rod inside the ark as an eternal memorial. This means that resurrection is an eternal principle in our service to God. A servant of the Lord is one who has died and resurrected. God testifies again and again to His people that authority to serve God lies in resurrection, not in a person himself. All services to the Lord must pass through death and resurrection before they will be acceptable to God. Resurrection means that everything is of God and not of us. It means that God alone is able and that we are not able. Resurrection means that everything is done by God, not by ourselves. All those who think highly of themselves and who hold a misguided judgment of themselves have never realized what resurrection is. No one should be mistaken to think that he can do anything by himself. If a man continues to think that he is able, that he can do something, and that he is useful, he does not know resurrection. He may know the doctrine of resurrection, the reason for resurrection, or the result of resurrection, but he does not know resurrection. All those who know resurrection have given up hope in themselves; they know that they cannot make it. As long as the natural strength remains, the power of resurrection has no ground for manifestation. As long as Sarah could beget a child, Isaac would not come. What we can do belongs to the natural realm, and what is impossible for us to do belongs to the realm of resurrection.

God's ability is not manifested in His creation but in resurrection. God's greatest power is manifested not through creation but through resurrection. When God's power is manifested in creation, it does not need to be preceded by death. But when His power is manifested in resurrection, there is the need for it to be preceded by death. Every created thing needs no precedence for its creation, but everything in resurrection has its precedence. If a man can survive by what he possessed in the first place, he has not experienced any resurrection. If a man's ability is according to what he had in the first place, he does not have resurrection. If he is what he was in the first place, he does not have resurrection. If what he has is what he possessed in the first place, he does not have resurrection. We must acknowledge that we can do nothing, are nothing, and have nothing. We are like a dead dog. If we acknowledge this, and we find that something is still alive in us, that is resurrection. Creation does not require the knowledge of death, but resurrection requires that we fall down, prostrate before God, and confess to Him, "I can do nothing. I am nothing, and I have nothing. This is what I am. If I can give anything to others, it is because You have given it to me. If I can do anything, it is because You have done it through me." Once we prostrate before the Lord in this way, everything we have will become God's work in us. Henceforth, we will never be mistaken. We will realize that everything that is dead belongs to us and everything that is living belongs to God. We have to separate ourselves from the Lord clearly; everything that has to do with death belongs to us, and everything that has to do with life belongs to the Lord. The Lord is never confused, but we are often confused. A man must come to the end of himself before he will be convinced of his utter uselessness. After Sarah gave birth to Isaac, she would never be foolish enough to think that her own strength was responsible for it. The colt would not be mistaken to think that the hosannas were directed at it. God has to bring us to the point where we will no longer be confused about what is of God and what is of us.

Everyone who is an authority should know this; he should not be mistaken in any way. There must be no misunderstanding with authority. Authority is of God and not of us; we are only those who keep custody of authority. Only those who have seen this are qualified to be a deputy authority. Brothers and sisters, when you set out for your work, I hope that none of you would be foolish enough to think that you have any authority in yourself. As soon as you offend the principle of resurrection, you lose authority, and as soon as you try to exhibit your authority, you instantly lose authority. A dry rod can exhibit nothing but death. But when you have resurrection, you have authority, because authority rests with resurrection, not with the natural life. Everything that we have is natural. Hence authority does not rest in us but in the Lord.

THE TREASURE AND THE EARTHEN VESSEL

Paul's word in 2 Corinthians 4:7 matches the teaching here. I have often thought that Paul painted a wonderful picture in that chapter. He compared himself to an earthen vessel, one made of clay. He compared the power of resurrection within him to a treasure. This is like the precious ointment in the alabaster box. He knew very well that he himself was just an earthen vessel. But the treasure within him constituted the excellency of power. There is a vast difference between these two things. Paul said that this resurrection power is a treasure and that it is a surpassingly great power. This is truly the word of an honest man; he said it like it was—"the excellency of the power." Following this he said that he was pressed on every side, but that he was not constricted because of the efficacy of the treasure. In himself he could not find a way out, but with the treasure he was not utterly without a way out. In himself he was persecuted, but with the treasure he was not abandoned. In himself he was cast down, but with the treasure he was not destroyed. As far as he was concerned, he was pressed on every side. But as far as the treasure was concerned, he was not constricted. On the one hand, there is death, but on the other hand, there is life. On the one hand, we have a constant deliverance to death, but on the other hand, we have the producing of life. Death operates on the one hand, and life is manifested on the other hand. Second Corinthians 4 and 5 unfold the center of Paul's ministry. Here we find the principle of death and resurrection and nothing else. Everything in us is death, and everything in the Lord is resurrection.

AUTHORITY BEING WHERE RESURRECTION IS

If there is any authority in us, this authority comes from God, not from us. We should never be mistaken. We should see clearly that all authority comes from the Lord. We are here on earth merely to maintain His authority; we are not here to maintain our own authority. Authority does not belong to us. Whenever we trust in the Lord, we see authority. Whenever we express the natural life, we become the same as everyone else, and there is no authority in us whatsoever. Only that which issues from resurrection results in authority. Authority is based on resurrection, not on ourselves. No ordinary rod can be placed before God. Only a rod of resurrection can be placed before Him. Furthermore, resurrection is found in the budding rod. It is not a general resurrection but a full resurrection. It is not just a faint expression of the resurrection life but a life that has budded, blossomed, and brought forth fruit. This is resurrection life in maturity. Only one matured in resurrection life can act as God's deputy authority. The more resurrection life is expressed through us, the more authority we will have.

CHAPTER SIXTEEN

THE MISUSE OF DEPUTY AUTHORITY AND GOD'S GOVERNMENTAL JUDGMENT

Scripture Reading: Num. 20:2-3, 7-13, 22-28; Deut. 32:48-52

A DEPUTY AUTHORITY SHOULD SANCTIFY THE LORD

After the Israelites wandered in the wilderness for over thirty years, we find in Numbers 20 that they forgot the lesson that they had learned through their rebellion. When they came into the wilderness of Zin, they were without water, and they murmured and spoke against Moses and Aaron (vv. 2-3). Moses and Aaron had learned many lessons before the Lord already. But this time Moses erred in acting as God's deputy authority. We need to consider how God judges a deputy authority when he fails. God was not angry this time at the people's murmuring; He told Moses to take the rod, which was a symbol of God's authority, and to speak to the rock so that it might yield its water. This shows that Moses and Aaron were God's deputy authority. God did not say that He wanted to punish the Israelites. Moses and Aaron were not young men, yet they still failed in their position as God's deputy authority. Verse 10 shows that Moses was very angry when he said, "Hear now, you rebels; shall we bring forth water for you out of this rock?" The phrase *you rebels* is strong in English as well as in Hebrew. It is a short expression in Hebrew. Moses used very strong words. He was angry. He might have thought, "This rebellious people has been causing trouble for decades, and they are causing trouble still." He forgot God's command and struck the rock with the rod twice. Although Moses was wrong, water flowed out just the same (v. 11).

This act prompted God to rebuke His servant. He said, "You did not believe in Me, to sanctify Me in the eyes of the sons of Israel" (v. 12a). This means that Moses and Aaron had not sanctified God; they had not separated God from themselves. Moses' speaking was wrong and his striking was also wrong. His spirit was completely wrong, and he represented God in a wrong way. In reading the Bible we have to touch the spirit of the Word. It seems that God was saying, "I saw that My people were thirsty, and I gave them to drink. Why are you rebuking them?" God said that Moses and Aaron had not sanctified Him. This means that they had not set Him apart as the holy One. It seems that God was saying, "You have involved Me in your errors." A person's words have to do with his attitude. Moses' word did not sanctify God. His attitude was different from God's attitude, and his feeling different from God's feeling. God did not rebuke the people, but Moses did. This caused the Israelites to misunderstand God. They thought that God was fierce, that He was quick to condemn, and that He was a merciless God.

It is imperative that an authority represent God properly. Whether in wrath or in compassion, he should be like God all the time. If we are wrong, we should confess that we are wrong; we should never drag God into our mistake. If we do, we will bring judgment upon ourselves. We must be careful. It is a serious thing to drag God into our mistakes. Moses had been a deputy authority for decades, but he implicated God in his error. He represented God wrongly. This is why God had to judge him. When a deputy authority makes a mistake and does not confess it, God will step forward to vindicate Himself. It would be wrong for God to not judge Moses and Aaron. God's dealing with Moses and Aaron meant that this act was committed by Moses and Aaron only, and that God had no part in it. Israel's murmuring could have been a rebellion in attitude only; their spirit might have been different. This is why God did not judge them. Moses should not have judged them rashly when God had not judged them. He should not have uttered any unrestrained words according to himself. Moses rebuked the Israelites. This was his own attitude and his own wrath. But this easily could have lead the Israelites to believe that this was God's attitude and God's wrath. Man's wrath does not accomplish the righteousness of God. This is why God needed to vindicate Himself. He had to separate Himself from Moses and Aaron. He had to show the whole world that what Moses did that day was done by Moses alone; it was not done by Him. The words Moses spoke on that day were his own words; they were not God's words. We can never implicate God in our mistakes or our personal failures, or give others the impression that our attitude is the attitude that God is expressing through His deputy authority. If we do, God will have to vindicate Himself. A deputy authority acts on behalf of God. If *we* become angry, we can only say that *we* are angry, that it is *we* who are behind it, not God. We have to separate the two. My worst fear is that man would become so bold as to associate his own acts with God's work, and think it unnecessary to identify his actions as his own.

We are too prone to errors. Once we make a mistake, we should acknowledge it. On the one hand, this will save us from wrongly representing God and falling into the evil one's ensnarement. On the other hand, this will save us from falling into darkness. If we take the lead to acknowledge our mistakes, God will not have to vindicate Himself. Otherwise, we will fall into God's governmental hand.

THE SERIOUSNESS OF BEING A DEPUTY AUTHORITY

The result of this incident was the manifestation of God's judgment. God said that Moses and Aaron could no longer enter the land of Canaan on account of their mistake (v. 12b). When man speaks and acts loosely and does not sanctify God, He will vindicate Himself. When this happens, man can no longer ask God for forgiveness. Here is another thing that we should note: Every time we execute God's authority and take care of His business, we have to do it with fear and trembling. We cannot let down our guard or become presumptuous just because we have become old. When Moses was angry and threw down God's handwritten tablets of stone, God did not judge him because he was filled with God's jealousy, and it was right for him to do that. He was zealous for God, and God did not rebuke him. But after following God for so many

years, he misrepresented God by disobeying Him, striking
the rock twice, and speaking rash words. He had incriminated
God in his mistakes, and he had dragged God into his error.
He made others think that his words were God's words and
his judgments God's judgments. This was a grave error. In
order to serve God, we must sanctify Him, and we must not
associate Him with ourselves loosely. Otherwise, when God
vindicates Himself, we will suffer severe judgment. Moses
lost his right to enter Canaan through this one mistake.

GOD'S GOVERNMENTAL JUDGMENT

The Israelites could not enter Canaan because they had
rebelled many times. Moses and Aaron were wrong only once.
Yet they could not enter Canaan either. It is a sobering thing
to be a deputy authority. God's judgment on a deputy authority is serious. In Numbers 18 God told Aaron that he and his
sons would bear the iniquity of the sanctuary (v. 1). The more
a person represents God's authority, the more God scrutinizes
him and will not let him go. In Luke 12 the Lord also said,
"To every one to whom much has been given, much will be
required from him; and to whom much has been committed,
they will ask of him all the more" (v. 48).

Numbers 20 tells us that Aaron would die on Mount Hor
through this judgment. We see Moses, Aaron, and his son
Eleazar going up Mount Hor together (vv. 25-27). What a
beautiful picture this is! All three were submissive and willingly accepted God's judgment. They really knew God. This
is why they did not even pray. Aaron knew that his day had
come, and Moses also knew what was to become of himself.
They were like Abraham when he took Isaac up the mountain. Abraham knew Isaac's future. God told Moses to take
Aaron and Eleazar with him up to the mountain, because
in the incident by the waters of Meribah, Moses was the
one who took the lead. On the mountain Moses found the way
that Aaron was to take, and he also found the way he would
take.

As soon as Aaron's garments were stripped off, he died
(v. 28). Ordinarily, when a man takes off his garments, he
does not die. But when Aaron's garments were removed, he

died. This means that his life was derived from his service. It means that when a servant of the Lord ceases his service, his life stops. There are many people who are not genuine servants. When they cease their so-called service, their life continues to go on. Here we see that Aaron was a genuine servant of the Lord.

Deuteronomy 32 shows us that God's judgment does not go away with time. God dealt with Moses in the same way that He dealt with Aaron. He told Moses to go up to Mount Nebo and die there (vv. 48-52). During those years Moses was faithful. Deuteronomy 32 and 33 tell us that before he died, he sang to and blessed the children of Israel. He did not pray for God to spare him from such a judgment. He humbly and meekly submitted to the hand of God. Even though he was a deputy authority of God who was obedient to God all his life, he was barred from entering Canaan because of his one failure in representing God. What a great loss this was! Moses was brought up to Mount Nebo to the peak of Pisgah. Nebo was the plateau, while Pisgah was the peak. There God told Moses, "This is the land which I swore to Abraham, to Isaac, and to Jacob, saying, To your seed I will give it. I have let you see it with your own eyes, but you will not go over there" (34:4). God's promise lasted for five hundred years from the time of Abraham, but Moses could only see it; he could not inherit it, because he misrepresented God's authority by the waters of Meribah. What a loss he suffered!

I have a very heavy burden which I want to share with you. Nothing is more serious and sobering than to misrepresent authority. I am fearful that our young brothers would wrongly represent God's authority. We may be wrong only once, but that one mistake can bring in God's judgment. Every time we execute God's authority, we have to pray that we are joined to God. The minute we make a mistake, we have to learn to separate ourselves from God. Otherwise we will bring God's judgment upon ourselves. In making a decision we have to ask if the decision is according to God's will. We can say that we are acting in His name only if we know for sure that it is God's will. Moses rebuked the Israelites and struck the rock by the waters of Meribah. He could not say that he was acting in the name of the Lord. He should have said, "I am doing this by myself." Otherwise, he would bring judgment on himself. I hope that you will not be foolish but will learn to live before the Lord in fear and trembling. Do not act or walk rashly when you say that you are doing things in the name of the Lord. Do not pass on careless judgments or make proposals easily. Control your spirit and your tongue. In particular, shut your mouth when you are angry. When you act as God's deputy authority, you will either do a good job or you will drag God into your error. This is a serious matter. The more a man knows God, the more careful he will be. If you fall into God's governmental hand, you may be forgiven at times, but you may not be forgiven at other times. No one can touch or offend God's government. We have to be clear about this way. Only after we have seen the proper way of representing authority can we be a deputy authority.

A DEPUTY AUTHORITY
CANNOT AFFORD TO MAKE A MISTAKE

Self-motivated service cannot find acceptance in the eyes of God. In fact, no one can render any service at all by himself. A man must serve by standing on the ground of resurrection before his service can be approved. The Lord does not want us to be misguided to assume that authority comes from someone other than God. We are not the authority; we are only here to represent authority. The flesh has no place. We must also tell others that everything wrong comes from us and everything right comes from God. Every time we talk to men or deal with matters, we have to remember that we cannot trust in ourselves and that we have to understand God's will. We cannot go out on our own and make suggestions or decisions lightly. Authority does not rest with us; we are merely the deputy authorities. If we act according to our own will, we will create big problems. The church cannot be without authority, and the church cannot tolerate the misuse of authority. God has only one mind, which is to build up His own authority.

In the church submission to authority is absolute, and fear and trembling on the part of the deputy authority should also be absolute. Without submission there is no church. At the same time, a deputy authority must not make suggestions or decisions loosely, and he must not speak carelessly or dictate others' pathways. It is wrong to judge the brothers or to interpret the Bible lightly. Our submission must be absolute, and our representation of authority must also be absolute. There are two problems in the church today. One is the lack of absolute submission, and the other is the misrepresentation of authority. We must learn not to speak loosely or make proposals casually. Our spirit has to be open to the Lord all the time, and we have to look to His light. If we do not, we will implicate God in our mistakes. We may even say that we are acting in the Lord's name or on His behalf. Actually, none of our actions are of the Lord. We must learn to submit on the one hand, and learn to represent God on the other hand. Hence, we must know the cross, and we must know resurrection. Whether or not the church will have a way to go on depends on how we have learned this lesson.

AUTHORITY BEING BASED ON MINISTRY, AND MINISTRY BEING BASED ON RESURRECTION

A man's authority is based on his ministry, and his ministry is based on resurrection. Without resurrection there is no ministry, and without ministry there is no authority. Without resurrection, Aaron could not serve. His service was based on resurrection, and his authority before men was also based on resurrection. Resurrection enables us to serve before God and establishes us as an authority before men. God will never appoint a man who has no ministry to be His authority.

Authority today is not a matter of position. Without a spiritual service, there cannot be any positional authority. Only after a man has a spiritual service before the Lord can he have authority before men. This means that God will appoint you as an authority among His children only after you have acquired a spiritual ministry. Hence, authority is based on one's ministry before God, and ministry is based on resurrection. For this reason, there is no dispute in the matter of authority, for there is no dispute in the matter of ministry. Ministry is something given by God. Hence, authority is also something decided by God. If a ministry has not been given to you, no authority has been assigned to you. All authority is based on service. Without service there is no authority. Aaron had authority because he had a service before the Lord. His censer could make propitiation and stop the plague, while the censers of the other 250 leaders were cursed by God. The rebellion in Numbers 16 was not only a rebellion against authority, but a rebellion against ministry. Aaron had a spiritual ministry because he was in resurrection. He was able to be the authority because he had such a ministry.

We should not have any authority that extends beyond our ministry. No one can acquire an authority that goes beyond his ministry. We should not boast of any authority that is apart from our ministry. We have to learn to be faithful in our ministry before the Lord and faithful in our authority before men. We should have the attitude that we will not go about in things too great or too wondrous for us (Psa. 131:1). We have to learn to be faithful to our portion before the Lord. Many people make the mistake of thinking that anyone can assume authority. Little do they realize that any authority which issues from a ministry never goes beyond its own service to rule over God's children. Your measure of authority before men must match your ministry before God. The amount of service you have before God determines the amount of authority you have before men. As soon as authority goes beyond ministry, it becomes a positional authority, and it is no longer spiritual.

Authority issues from ministry, and when it flows to others, it brings the presence of God with it. Ministry grows out of resurrection and is rooted in God. If a minister misrepresents authority, his ministry will stop, just as Moses' and Aaron's ministries were stopped. We have to learn to maintain the Lord's authority and not to say things loosely. Otherwise, we will suffer God's judgment.

GOD'S VINDICATION

When a deputy authority makes a mistake, God will step forward to judge it. His judgment is His vindication. God's vindication is one great principle in His administration. God is willing to commit His name to us; He has allowed us to use His name, just as a man commits his personal seal to another and allows the latter to use it in his name. This being the case, when we misrepresent God, He will have to vindicate Himself. God needs to show man that the mistake is caused by us and not by Him.

Moses and Aaron suffered serious judgment as a result of one mistake. In the end Aaron died and Moses also died. The greater loss though was their disqualification from entering Canaan. Neither one of them debated with God; they knew that God's vindication was more important than their entry into Canaan. They were willing to allow God to vindicate Himself rather than enter Canaan. In Deuteronomy 32 Moses especially made the point that they, rather than God, had made the mistake. We must maintain the absoluteness of the truth; we should not try to take any shortcuts. No faithful servant of God should take the cheap way out. God's vindication is more important than our face, our likes, and our years of prayers and hopes. Moses and Aaron were meek; they submitted to the hand of God. They could have reasoned with God, but they chose, rather, to not argue. They did not pray for themselves even to the end. They prayed many times for the children of Israel, but they did not pray for themselves. Such silence is precious. They knew how to let God vindicate Himself, and they willingly took the blame upon themselves. When Moses wrote of this in his book, he pointed out that he was the one who made the mistake. We thank the Lord because here was a servant who knew how to judge himself and who allowed God to vindicate Himself. He did not argue in the face of judgment. He did not make proposals lightly and he did not want to control others. He was humble and gracious, and he feared God. He is indeed a model for us who are serving the Lord.

May the Lord give us the grace to be a teachable person. May He be gracious to the church in this end time. We need to pray, "Lord, may Your authority be manifested in the church, and may every brother and sister know what authority is. May authority be manifested in the local church, and may deputy authority be manifested through man." I hope that the responsible ones in the church will not make any mistake concerning the matter of authority, and I hope that there will also be no mistake on the part of those who receive orders from the authority. I hope that everyone will know where he stands so that the Lord will have a free way to go on.

CHAPTER SEVENTEEN

THE NEED FOR A DEPUTY AUTHORITY TO SUBMIT TO AUTHORITY

Scripture Reading: 1 Sam. 24:1-6; 26:7-12; 2 Sam. 1:5-15; 2:1; 4:5—5:3; 6:16-23; 7:18; 15:19-20, 24-26; 16:5-14; 19:9-15

In the Old Testament David was the second king appointed by God. Before David there was Saul, who was also appointed by God. David was the up-to-date authority appointed by God; he was God's present anointed one. Saul was God's displaced authority; he was God's previous anointed one. God's Spirit left Saul, but he was still on the throne. David was already appointed the king, yet Saul would not step down. What should David do? Here we see how David submitted to authority and how he did not build up his own authority. David was a man according to God's heart. He could be a deputy authority because he was a person who genuinely submitted to authority.

WAITING FOR GOD TO ESTABLISH AUTHORITY

First Samuel 24 tells us of a story in the wilderness in Engedi. Saul was pursuing David. When David hid in a cave, Saul went into the same cave to cover his feet. David was hiding in the innermost part of the cave. He cut off a corner of Saul's cloak, but later rebuked himself (vv. 4b-5). His conscience was very tender and keen. First Samuel 26 tells us of another opportunity that David had to kill Saul. This time, however, he only took his spear and water jug (v. 12a). David cut off a corner of Saul's cloak and took something in his possession. This could have served very well as a basis for him to boast to Saul (vv. 17-20). But this would have been the way of a lawyer, not the way of a Christian. A lawyer is only concerned with reason and evidence. But a Christian is concerned with feeling; he is not concerned with reason. He is concerned with fact, not with evidence. David had the sense and feeling of a Christian. This is why he rebuked himself after he cut off a corner of Saul's cloak. We should be those who are only concerned with facts before the Lord; we are not for politics. We should not pay attention merely to the procedures. Both in Shanghai and Foochow I have seen brothers who were concerned only with procedures and evidence. But here was a man who began to rebuke himself after he had only cut Saul's cloak. A Christian is one who is concerned with inward feeling, not with proof of evidence. Those in the world are concerned with proof of evidence. A person may be able to cut the cloak of others, he may be able to take their spear and water jug, and he may be able to boast of it, but his heart will condemn him. David was a person who could submit to authority. He did not tear down Saul's authority. Instead he waited for God to establish his authority. He was able to wait; he did not try to "help" God by hastening Saul's death. A deputy authority of God must learn not to establish his own authority, but to build up the authority of those who are over him.

NOT BEING GOD'S CHOICE ALONE, BUT ALSO THE CHURCH'S CHOICE

Second Samuel tells us of a person who came to David and reported that he had killed Saul. He thought that he would be rewarded, but David killed him instead. The man was wrong because he had annulled God's authority (1:10-15). Although he had not annulled David, David felt that it was wrong that the man had annulled Saul's authority. He judged any annulment of authority.

After Saul died, David asked God to which city he should go. At that time the palace was in Gibeah. Who among the Israelites did not know David? As soon as David knew of Saul's death, he should have gone to the capital with his warriors. Humanly speaking, he should have hurried to Gibeah with his army. This was a golden moment. How could he let it slip away? As far as common sense goes, he should have gone up to Gibeah. It was good enough that he had been submissive. Who did not know that David was a warrior? But he acted strangely. He inquired of God, and God told him to go to Hebron (2:1). Hebron was a small city and an unimportant one. At that time some came from Judah and anointed him the king of Judah. This shows us that David did not try to seize authority by himself. He left it up to God's people to anoint him (v. 4). When Samuel anointed him, it was a mark that God had chosen him. When the people anointed him, it was a mark that God's people (a type of the church) had chosen him. David could not deny or reject the men of Judah's anointing. He could not say, "Since I have God's anointing already, why do I need your anointing?" It is one thing for God to anoint someone, and it is another thing for His people to anoint someone. A deputy authority must be not only God's choice but the church's choice as well. No one can impose his authority upon others. He must wait for God's children to make their choice.

David did not go up to Gibeah. Rather, he waited for God's people to come to him in Hebron. He waited for seven years and six months. Seven and a half years is not a short time. But David was not in any hurry. I have not seen one person who was full of self and desirous of self-glory who also was chosen by God to be an authority. God anointed David not only as the king of Judah but also as the king over the whole nation of Israel. Yet as long as God's people did not acknowledge him, he would not come forward. When only the house of Judah anointed him, he was satisfied to just be the king of Judah. He was not in any haste. He could wait.

After seven and a half years, all the tribes of Israel came to Hebron and spoke to David, saying, "Here we are; we are your bone and your flesh. Even previously, when Saul was king over us, it was you who led out and brought in Israel. And Jehovah said to you, You shall shepherd My people Israel, and you shall be ruler over Israel" (5:1-2). The tribe of Judah first acknowledged him as king in Hebron. After seven years and six months, the elders of the tribes of Israel anointed him as king, and then he reigned in Jerusalem for thirty-three years. In David we see that authority is not self-appointed. It is not imposed upon others. Authority is appointed by God

and anointed by men. An authority does not proclaim himself
the king, and he is not just appointed by God to be king. First,
he is chosen by God, and then he is acknowledged by man.
David was a real king. In the New Testament, when David is
spoken of, he is addressed as "David the king" (Matt. 1:6),
but Solomon is not addressed as a king. The New Testament
gives special recognition to David's kingship because he did
not trust in himself. He had God's anointing, and he waited
for the anointing of His people, that is, the church.

We should have not only the Lord's anointing but also the
church's anointing before we assume authority among His
children. David waited from the age of thirty to thirty-seven.
He did not doubt. He did not say, "What will happen if the
children of Israel do not anoint me?" He was humbled under
the hand of God. Everyone who knows God can wait. Those
who know God do not need to move a finger to help themselves. If you are in the right condition, not only will the
Lord acknowledge you as His representative; the church also
will acknowledge you as God's representative. I hope that you
will have not only God's anointing but the church's anointing
as well. You must never contend with your flesh or try to
move your finger. The flesh has no place here. No one can
stand up to proclaim, "I am God's appointed authority. You
must all obey me." We must first learn to have a spiritual
ministry before the Lord. We must wait for God's time before
we can serve Him among His children.

THE MORE A PERSON IS AN AUTHORITY, THE MORE HE UPHOLDS AUTHORITY

David waited in Hebron for seven and a half years because
Ishbosheth, Saul's son, continued to be king in Mahanaim after
Saul's death (2 Sam. 2:8-9). Later Ishbosheth was assassi-
nated by Baanah and Rechab. They took his head to David
in Hebron, thinking that they were bringing good tidings to
David. But David killed them (4:5-12). He judged the rebellious
ones. This shows that the more a person is an authority, the
more he upholds authority. We cannot build up our own
authority at the expense of others' authority. The less a man
seeks for authority, the more God gives him authority. The

minute a person rebels against authority he should be judged, whether or not he is rebelling against your authority. When David did this, he gained the favor of God's people. Consequently, 2 Samuel 5 says that the eleven tribes sent men to seek after David. A man who knows God's authority is submissive to authority. Such a one is qualified to be an authority. You should not deal with anyone just because he has offended *your* authority. You have to wait for God's children to anoint you as the authority. Before the children of God anoint you, it is wrong to harbor any complaints or murmurings.

HAVING NO AUTHORITY BEFORE GOD

Second Samuel 6 says that when David brought God's ark back to the city of David, he danced before the ark with all his might. David was already king of the whole nation of Israel. When Michal the daughter of Saul saw this, she despised David (vv. 14-16). Michal thought that since David was the king, he should have sanctified himself in the eyes of the Israelites. Of course, it is right that a king should not be wild. But David was not wrong in what he saw. He saw that he had no authority before God, that he was lowly and worthless. Michal's mistake was her father's mistake. Saul kept the best of the cattle and the sheep; he disobeyed God's commandment and was rejected by God. Yet he tried to save his face by asking Samuel to recommend him before the people of Israel (see 1 Sam. 15:1-30). The way Michal took was different from the way David took. God was pleased with David, and He judged Michal. Michal had no descendant until the day of her death (2 Sam. 6:23). This means that God cut off any continuation of such a person. He would not allow such a person to go on.

When David went before the Lord, he felt that he was as lowly as anyone else; he did not consider himself higher than others. A deputy authority should take a place before God that is as equally low and humble as all the people of God. He should not exalt himself or try to uphold his authority among men. On his throne David was the king, but before the ark he was the same as all the children of Israel. They were all God's people and were all the same. Michal wanted to hold on to her way; she wanted David to be a king even before God. She could not stand David's action, and said to him, "How the king of Israel has made himself honorable today!" (v. 20). But God accepted David's way and judged Michal's way. When Moses went before the Lord, he was the same as the people of Israel. When David went before the Lord, he was also the same as the people of Israel. We may be an authority in the church, but when we go before the Lord, we are the same as everyone else. This is the basis and secret of an authority—being the same as all the brothers when he goes before the Lord.

HAVING NO CONSCIOUSNESS OF BEING AN AUTHORITY

I am particularly fond of one sentence in 2 Samuel 7:18: "Then King David went and sat before Jehovah." By then the temple was not yet built. The ark was in the tabernacle and David sat on the floor. God made a covenant with David, and David offered a wonderful prayer. Here we touch a pliable spirit, a sensitive spirit. Before David was king, he was a warrior, and no one was able to stand before him. Now that he had become king and his nation had become strong, he was meek enough to sit on the floor beside the ark. Here was a person who maintained his humility. He could pray in a very simple way. This is a picture of a deputy authority.

Michal, who was born in the palace, was concerned with pomp and majesty, like her father. She did not realize the difference between being sent by the Lord and entering into the presence of the Lord. When a man is sent by the Lord, he may have a certain degree of authority in speaking and acting on God's behalf. But once he enters the presence of the Lord, he has to fall down before His feet; he has to know who he is. David was indeed a king appointed by the Lord; he was endowed with the God-given authority. If we count Saul out, David was the first king appointed by God. Christ is not only the descendant of Abraham but also the descendant of David. The last name recorded in the whole Bible is the name of David (Rev. 22:16). However, the amazing thing is that though David was king, he did not have the consciousness that he was king. He knew that he was nothing in the eyes of the Lord. If a man is always conscious of his authority, he is not qualified to be an authority. An authority must learn to know himself. The more a person is an authority, the less consciousness he should have about his authority. God's deputy authority should have such a blessed ignorance—being an authority without having the consciousness of it.

NO NEED TO UPHOLD ONE'S AUTHORITY

Second Samuel 15 is a record of Absalom's rebellion. This was a double rebellion. On the one hand, it was the rebellion of a son against his father. On the other hand, it was the rebellion of a people against their king. This was the greatest rebellion David experienced. His son was taking the lead in this rebellion. At that time, more and more people were following Absalom, and David had to flee from the capital. He was in need of followers. Ittai the Gittite wanted to follow him, but David was able to say to Ittai, "Return and abide with the king" (v. 19). David was truly meek. His spirit was truly keen. He did not say, "I am the king, and all of you should follow me." Instead he told Ittai, "You can take your way. I have no intention to drag many people into my woes. Even if you choose to go to the new king, that is fine with me." He was in the midst of his tribulation, yet he still would not take people along with him. It is not easy to know a person when he lives in the palace. But when he is in the midst of trials, his true personality is manifested. Here David was not rash or careless. He was still humble and submissive.

After he crossed the brook Kidron, he was about to turn to the wilderness. Zadok the high priest with all the priests and the Levites wanted to come with him, and they took the ark along with them. If the ark had left the city, many Israelites would have gone with it. Zadok and the Levites' attitude was right: When rebellion broke out, they had to remove the ark. But at this juncture David did not say, "This is good. Do not leave the ark with the rebellious ones." David thought that if the ark left Jerusalem, many of the people of Israel would be in turmoil. He was a person who had ascended to a great height. He would not allow the ark to go with him.

He was willing to resign himself to God's dealing. His attitude was the same as that of Moses, who was altogether humbled under the mighty hand of God. Both of them ascended to a height that was unmatched by their opposers. David said that if he should find favor in the sight of the Lord, He would bring him back again to see the ark and His habitation. If he did not find favor in God's sight, it would have been useless even if the ark followed him. Therefore, he exhorted Zadok the high priest and the Levites who bore the ark to return (vv. 24-26). This was easy to say but difficult to do. There were not many people who escaped from Jerusalem, and the city was filled with rebellious ones. Now he had to send his good friends away. How pure was David's spirit! He was still humbling himself meekly before the Lord, just as Moses did.

In verse 27 David said to Zadok that since he was a priest and a seer, he should take the lead to bring the priests and the ark back. At that word the group returned. In reading this passage, we have to touch David's spirit. His spirit was saying, "Why do I have to fight with others? Whether or not I remain a king is God's business. I do not need many people to follow me, and I do not need the ark to accompany me." He realized that being an authority is God's business and that no one needs to maintain his own authority. David went up to the Mount of Olives, weeping as he went up and with his head covered (v. 30). Here indeed was a meek and pliable man! This was what David did when he was offended. He did not hold on to his authority. This is the proper attitude of a God-appointed authority.

AN AUTHORITY SHOULD HAVE THE CAPACITY
TO TAKE OFFENSE

A rebellious spirit is contagious. Second Samuel 16 tells us that Shimei came forth along the way. He threw stones at David and cursed him, saying that he had shed the blood of the house of Saul. Even David's followers suffered because of him. Nothing could be farther from the truth than Shimei's accusation. If there was a person who had not shed the blood of Saul's house, that person was David. Shimei could say that David had reigned in Saul's stead and that David was running for his life. There was nothing wrong in saying that. But it was a gross lie to say that David had shed the blood of Saul's house. Yet David did not argue. He did not vindicate himself or deny anything. David still had his mighty men with him, and it would have been easy for him to get rid of this man, but he would not do this. Shimei cursed as he went. Even David's followers could not stand it. Yet David exhorted them not to kill. He said, "Leave him alone and let him curse, for Jehovah has told him to do so" (v. 11). He was truly a broken and pliable man. He was learning to submit to a higher authority. David said that it was God who had told Shimei to curse him. In reading this portion of the Bible, we have to touch David's spirit. He was alone and an outcast. At least he could have taken out his frustration on Shimei and vindicated himself a little. However, he was an absolutely submissive person. He submitted absolutely to God and accepted everything that God had done to him.

Brothers and sisters, you must realize that God's appointed authority is one who can take offenses. He is one who can be offended. If the authority that you have received cannot suffer any offense, you are not qualified to be an authority. Do not think that you can act as you please as long as you have been given authority. Only those who have learned the lesson of obedience are qualified to be an authority. Verse 13 says that Shimei continued to curse David, yet David was truly a submissive man. Only such a person is qualified to be an authority. Here was a man who was truly pliable before the Lord. David and his followers rested wearily at a place. Even while Absalom was rebelling, David still maintained a proper attitude. He was a man in the Old Testament, yet he was full of the grace of the New Testament. He was so broken that he was able to have such a spirit. This is indeed a person who was qualified to be an authority.

LEARNING TO BE HUMBLED UNDER
THE MIGHTY HAND OF GOD

In 2 Samuel 19, after Absalom was defeated and killed, the Israelites heard that David was sitting in the city gate, and they all had fled to their own house (v. 8). David did not return with fanfare to his palace. Absalom had been anointed to be a king also. This was why David had to wait. The eleven tribes came and asked him to go back, but the tribe of Judah did not come along. David sent men to recover the tribe of Judah (vv. 9-12). David was of the tribe of Judah, and he was driven away by it. This was why he had to wait for the people to ask him back. He was God's appointed authority, but during his trial, he learned to humble himself under the mighty hand of God. He did not try to build up his own authority. He accepted the arrangements in the environment and was humbled under the mighty hand of God. He was not in any haste. He was a warrior himself, but he did not fight for himself. All the battles were fought for the Lord's people. In the past God's people had anointed him to be the king. In order to return to his kingship, he had to wait for God's people to anoint him once again.

All those whom God uses to be an authority should have the spirit of David. We should not say anything to defend ourselves. There is no need for us to say anything for ourselves. We should not act on our own. There is no need to move even a little finger to prove that we are chosen by God. We should trust, wait, and humble ourselves. We have to wait for God's timing. God will surely accomplish what He has set out to accomplish. The more submissive we are, the more we will learn to be an authority. The more we prostrate ourselves before the Lord, the more God will vindicate us. But if we try to speak for ourselves, fight for ourselves, and complain, we will destroy God's work. We have to learn to humble ourselves under the mighty hand of God. The more we try to be an authority in ourselves, the more we will walk down the wrong path. The way is clear before us. In the Old Testament the greatest authority was Moses, while among all the kings the greatest authority was David. Both behaved the same way in their capacity as deputy authorities. We have to touch these men's spirits before we can maintain God's authority.

CHAPTER EIGHTEEN

THE LIFE AND HEART
OF A DEPUTY AUTHORITY

Scripture Reading: Mark 10:35-45

DRINKING THE LORD'S CUP
AND PARTAKING OF HIS BAPTISM

When the Lord was on the earth, He rarely taught others how to be an authority. This is because His goal on earth was not to establish authority among men. Mark 10:35-45 contains the clearest teaching concerning how to be an authority. Anyone who wants to be an authority must read this passage; it is the Lord's own teaching. Here He shows us the way to be an authority. We know that the conversation was initiated by James and John; they wanted to sit on the right and left of the Lord in His glory. They knew that such a request was somewhat blunt, and they were too shy to mention it to the Lord directly. Instead they said, "We want You to do for us whatever we ask You" (v. 35). They said this to first secure a promise from the Lord. But the Lord did not answer them immediately. He asked, "What do you want Me to do for you?" (v. 36). Since He did not know what they wanted, He could not promise them anything. At this point they said, "Grant to us to sit, one on Your right and one on Your left, in Your glory" (v. 37). This request implies two things. First, they wanted to be near the Lord, and second, they wanted authority in glory. It was proper for them to desire to be near the Lord; such a request was properly directed. But that was not all they wanted; they wanted authority in glory as well. They wanted to be over the other ten disciples. What did the Lord say to them? First, He said that He did not know what they wanted Him to do. Then He said that even they themselves did not know what they were asking (v. 38a).

They thought that sitting on the right and the left was something that the Lord could grant or dispense to them. But the Lord told them that it was not that simple. They wanted to be near the Lord and to have authority. The Lord did not say that their request was wrong, nor did He say that it was wrong to desire to be at His right and left side. He told them that in order to be on His right and left, they had to drink of His cup and be baptized with His baptism. James and John thought that they would acquire the place merely by asking. But the Lord told them that it was not a matter of asking but a matter of drinking the cup and partaking of the baptism. This is not a matter of prayer. It is not a matter of trying to sit on the right or left side of the Lord. If one does not drink of the Lord's cup and is not baptized with His baptism, his asking is in vain. If a man does not drink of the Lord's cup and is not baptized with His baptism, he cannot be near Him nor can he have any authority. The Lord is not free to grant position and authority to anyone. Only those who drink His cup and are baptized with His baptism are given position and authority. Drinking and baptism are the foundation. If the foundation is wrong, there cannot be the right superstructure. Suppose a child goes up to the mountain to pick flowers and then plants the flowers back in the soil. Even though he thinks that he has planted a garden, the flowers have no roots. James and John were wrong in the root matters. In order to be near the Lord and have authority in glory, they needed to drink His cup and be baptized with His baptism. If the disciples did not drink His cup and were not baptized with His baptism, they could neither be near Him nor receive authority and position. This is something that they would understand shortly. This is something that has to do with today, not just with the future.

WHAT IS THE LORD'S CUP?

What is the Lord's cup? His cup carries only one meaning. When the Lord was in the garden of Gethsemane, a cup was before Him. It was God's cup of righteousness which He was to drink. Yet He prayed to the Father, saying, "If it is possible, let this cup pass from Me; yet not as I will, but as You will" (Matt. 26:39). Here we clearly find that the cup and God's will were two different things. At that moment the cup was the cup, and God's will was God's will; the two had not yet become one. The cup could be changed, but God's will could never be changed. The Lord was asking if the cup could pass. But He was not asking to avoid God's will. The cup could pass, but He was absolute to carry out God's will. The cup was not a necessity. It was not permanent but incidental. If the cup was not God's will, He was willing to let it pass. But if the cup was God's will, He would drink it. The Lord's attitude was clear: If it is God's will that I drink the cup, I will drink it. But if it is not His will that I drink the cup, I will not drink it. His word indeed draws out our worship. He could never reverse the order of His word. It would have been wrong for Him to pray the other way around. In other words, the one thing He insisted on in the garden was knowing whether or not the cup was God's will. Before the cup and God's will became one, it was all right for the Lord to pray as He did. In fact, He prayed this way three times (v. 44). But when He knew that the cup and God's will were one, He said to Peter outside the garden, "The cup which the Father has given Me, shall I not drink it?" (John 18:11). In the garden He could ask for the cup to be removed, because the cup and God's will had not yet become one. Outside the garden the cup and God's will were one. At this point the cup was different; it was something from the Father. This is why the Lord said, "The cup which the Father has given Me, shall I not drink it?"

Here we find the deepest spiritual lesson. The Lord was not hasty even when He was about to go to the cross. He only wanted to carry out God's will. He was not set on crucifixion. Although His crucifixion was crucial, it could not replace God's will. Although the Lord's crucifixion was the most important thing, He was still under God's will. Although the Lord came in order that He would become a propitiation for the sins of many, and although He came expressly to be crucified for men, the cross could never surpass God's will. He did not go to the cross simply because the cross was good and necessary for men's salvation. He did not come for the crucifixion but for doing God's will. He went to the cross only after He realized that God's will was the cross. He went to the cross for the simple reason that it was God's will. He was not crucified for the sake of crucifixion. God's will is higher than the cross. Hence, the Lord's crucifixion was not just a matter of the cross but a matter of doing God's will. He went to the cross because the Father wanted the crucifixion.

We can see that the cup is dispensable but God's will is indispensable. The Lord did not ask for God's will to be taken from Him. He had no direct relationship with the cross; it was only an indirect relationship. His direct relationship was with the will of God. This is why He prayed in the garden of Gethsemane for the cup to depart from Him. He wanted to walk in God's will. He chose God's will; He was not choosing the cross. Hence, the Lord's cup signifies His subjection to God's paramount authority. He prostrated Himself to choose God's will, and His only desire was to carry out His will. This is why He asked James and John, "Are you able to drink the cup which I drink?" (Mark 10:38). In other words, He was asking if they could prostrate themselves to choose God's will in the same way that He prostrated Himself before God to choose His will.

This is like Abraham's offering up of Isaac, which I spoke of earlier. In the end Abraham took Isaac back. Perhaps many people have offered up their Isaac. It becomes a problem to them when they are asked to take Isaac back. This seems to be a loss of face to them. Many people attach themselves directly to their consecration. Others attach themselves directly to suffering. Still others attach themselves directly to their work. But we should be directly attached to one thing only—God's will. To drink the Lord's cup means that we should not be attached directly to anything. If a cup is not God's will, we do not have to take it. Even though everyone knew that the Lord was going to go to the cross, He still prayed at the final hour to know whether the cross was God's will. Everything depends on God's will, not on us. Many people work for the sake of work itself. Once they take up a work, they cannot take up anything else. They are stuck to their work and sunk in their work. They have no more time to consider God's will. They insist on having their work to the end. This is not working for God's will but working for the sake of working. The Lord was so much for God's will that He was able even to give up the cross. When He understood God's will to be the cross, He took it without consideration of its pain. Drinking the cup means that we deny our own will and yield to God's will. The Lord was asking the disciples if they could yield to God's will in the same way that He yielded to God's will. This is the Lord's cup. If a man wants to be near the Lord or receive glory, he has to obey God's will.

Obedience to God's will is an important matter. It is a great matter. If a man can say glibly that he obeys God's will, he probably has not seen the great significance of God's will. Obeying God's will means being related to His will directly. Everything else can change. Even the cross, God's cup of wrath, can change. But God's will can never change. Man must forever be subject to God's authority before he can obey God's will. In reading the prayer in Gethsemane, we have to touch this spirit. The garden of Gethsemane speaks of the peak of the Lord's submission on earth. He did not impose God's will on the cup. Here is a profound principle. God's will was the object of His submission; God's cup was not the object. From the first day to the last, Christ's unswerving allegiance was to the will of God. He obeyed God's will all the way to the end. This was more important for Him than anything else. I believe there is a most profound revelation in the Lord's earthly experience of Gethsemane. We have to know Christ Himself through such a deep experience. Up until a few hours before the cross, He was still not committed to the work of the cross; He was only committed to obedience to God's will. Hence, the highest calling is not the work, the suffering, or the cross, but the will of God. This is why the Lord asked James and John, "Are you able to drink the cup which I drink?" It seems that the Lord was saying, "If a man wants to draw near to Me and receive a place in glory above that of the other children of God, he must be like Me, yielding to God's will and taking it as the unique goal. Only such ones can come near to Me and sit at My right and left hand." Whether or not we can be near the Lord and sit at His right and left depends on whether we can drink His cup, which is to render absolute obedience to His will.

WHAT IS THE LORD'S BAPTISM?

What is the Lord's baptism? Clearly the baptism that the Lord referred to was not the baptism at the river Jordan, because that was over. The baptism that the Lord was about to go through was forthcoming, referring to His death on the cross. In Luke 12:50 the Lord said, "I have a baptism to be baptized with, and how I am pressed until it is accomplished!" In his book *The Release of the Lord,* Mr. Austin-Sparks said that this refers to the Lord's desire to release Himself. The Lord was yearning to release Himself. The word *pressed* means confined or constricted. Christ had a sanctified body in which all of God's riches were embodied. Such glorious riches were bound by the flesh, and how constricted and confined He was! How wonderful it would be if these riches would be released! It seems as if He was saying that God's life was too confined and constricted within Him, and that it would be wonderful if it could be released. On the one hand, the cross was for redemption of sins. On the other hand, it was for the release of life. God released His life through the cross. The Lord desired that this life be released. Before crucifixion, however, such a life was constricted within Him. Hence, the basic and primary meaning of this baptism is the release of life.

Following this, the Lord said that once God's life was released, it would be kindled like fire on the earth. What would be the result of this baptism? It would result in something like a fire, something that would bring in division rather than peace on earth (v. 51). Once a fire touches something, it burns. From that time on, houses would be against houses, believers would be against unbelievers, those who have life would be against those who do not have life, and those with the fire would be against those without the fire. This is what it means to be baptized with the Lord's baptism.

Once life is released, let go, and unleashed, there will be division. Wherever this life goes, it will not bring peace, but strife. Some know the Lord and some do not know the Lord, and there will be strife. Once life enters a house, there will be striving in the house. Those who have passed through this baptism are immediately separated from those who have not passed through it. The Lord was saying, "I am going to the cross to release My life. This will bring in strife. Can you handle this? Do you like this?" First there is death, and then there is the release of life. This is baptism. The result of this baptism is division. Dead men cannot strive with one another; only those who have life can strive. The Lord's word points to the fact that death operates in us and life operates in others (2 Cor. 4:12). The Lord's baptism was the removal of the outward shell and the liberation of His life through death. This is what we are doing today. We must break the outward shell before the life within us can flow out.

When we were at Custom Lane [Translator's note: In Foochow at the base of Kuling Mountain], I mentioned that life cannot be released unless the outward man is first broken. Our outward man has constricted His life and restricted it from flowing out. We must realize that if the outward man is not broken, life cannot flow out. Once a man's outward shell is broken, he becomes very approachable and life flows out easily. Otherwise, life is bound; man's spirit is not released, and life does not flow freely. It is one thing to expound 2 Corinthians 4:12. It is altogether another thing to give others a touch of life. Many people think that this verse is merely a teaching. Let me repeat: Unless your outward man is broken, no life will flow out. Once a man's outward shell is broken, he becomes very approachable. This is like a grain of wheat that falls into the ground; the life within breaks forth from its shell and spontaneously grows out of the opening. This is what the Lord said in John 12:24: "Unless the grain of wheat falls into the ground and dies, it abides alone; but if it dies, it bears much fruit." When a grain of wheat falls to the ground, the shell breaks, and the life is released. Following this the Lord said, "He who loves his soul-life loses it; and he who hates his soul-life in this world shall keep it unto eternal life. If anyone serves Me, let him follow Me; and where I am, there also My servant will be. If anyone serves Me, the Father will honor him" (vv. 25-26). If a man wants to save his "shell," he will not be able to release the life. Once a man loses his "shell," he will bear much fruit.

There are two aspects to the cross—the aspect of redemption and the aspect of life-releasing. In Mark 10:35-45 the Lord did not speak of His *death;* He only spoke of His *baptism,* because He did not want others to think that James and John could participate in His redemptive work. The work of redemption can be accomplished only by Christ our High Priest; no one else can participate in it or do anything about it. We have no share in the Lord's death on the cross as far as redemption goes. But we do have a share in the release of His life. This is why the Lord only brought out the aspect of death that is related to His baptism when He spoke of the cross. This death has to do with the release of His life; it has nothing to do with redemption. The Lord said that He was going to go through a baptism. This meant that His outward shell would be broken and life would be released, like a grain of wheat breaking its shell and bearing much fruit. For a person to be baptized with the Lord's baptism means for him to be broken and torn down before the Lord and for life to come forth. If the outward man is not broken, it is very difficult for the Lord's life to be released. You may have life within you, but it cannot come out. You may be sitting very close to another person, but the life within you cannot come out or touch him.

The result of baptism is fire and division. Once this life flows out, there is no peace on earth. Instead, there is division. Many people are divided by this life. There is a big chasm between those who follow the Lord and those who do not. There is also a big difference between those who belong to the Lord and those who do not. Once a man touches the life of Christ, he takes a different way. There is much contention between those who have the Lord and those who do not, those who know God and those who do not, those who pay the price and those who do not, those who are faithful and those who are not, and those who accept the trials and those who do not. The Lord seemed to be saying, "Are you willing to bear the consequence of taking My baptism? You want to be on My right and left; you want to be different. But are you willing to bear the consequence of taking My baptism and becoming different from other children of God today?" In order to sit at the Lord's right and left and to have a place of glory, we have to drink His cup and be baptized with His baptism, which means that we have to acknowledge God's will above everything, to break the outward shell, and to release life. Only such ones know what it is to sit at the right and left of the Lord. This is the Christian pathway.

The Lord's word to James and John, in effect, was, "You must first drink My cup and pass through My baptism before you can sit on My right and left in glory. Can you drink this cup and be baptized with this baptism?" They answered, "We are able" (10:39). The two inquired of the Lord, but they did not know how serious their request was. They were not the only ones; all descendants of Adam are the same. The Lord spelled out the conditions, and they said that they were able. The Lord told them the fact, that to sit on His right and left required that they drink His cup and be baptized with His baptism. But even in saying this, He did not promise them His right and left side. What He meant was that if a man does not drink His cup and is not baptized with His baptism, he will surely not be able to sit on His right or left. But even if they drank His cup and passed through His baptism, they still might not sit on His right or left, because the latter depends on God's preparation (v. 40). If a man does not drink the Lord's cup and is not baptized with His baptism, he will surely not be able to sit on His right or left side. But even if he drinks His cup and is baptized with His baptism, he may still not be able to sit on His right or left side. Those who do not drink the Lord's cup and are not baptized with His baptism will surely not sit on His right or left. But those who drink His cup and are baptized with His baptism may not necessarily sit on His right or left. Perhaps James and John would ask, "What then can we say?" If one does not drink the cup and take the baptism, he is disqualified for sure. And if one drinks the cup and takes the baptism, he may be qualified, but it still depends on God's preparation. James and John could be off the mark in their request, but the Lord could not be inaccurate in His answer. If the Lord gave the right and left places to James and John, these two seats would have been gone for the past two thousand years of church history. Other seats might still be available, but these two seats would have been taken over by these two; they would have become reserved seats for the two disciples, and others would have been discouraged to go on in the Lord's way. The Lord did not grant their request, and the two seats are still available. Some among us may still have a chance to take those two seats. Therefore, this lesson is still applicable to us. But the main point of this passage is not in the preceding discussion but in what follows.

AN AUTHORITY DOES NOT DOMINATE OR CONTROL, BUT HUMBLES HIMSELF TO SERVE

Following this, the Lord talked about authority. Verse 41 says that when the other ten disciples heard about James and John's request, they became indignant. It appears that James and John asked the Lord in secret, but later the ten disciples found this out. Subsequently, the Lord taught them. Here is the subject of the whole passage. He gathered the disciples around and taught them things concerning the future glory. He said, "You know that those who are esteemed as rulers of the Gentiles lord it over them, and their great ones exercise authority over them. But it is not so among you; but whoever wants to become great among you shall be your servant, and whoever wants to be first among you shall be the slave of all. For even the Son of Man did not come to be served, but to serve and to give His life as a ransom for many" (vv. 42-45). The two disciples' question led to a discussion on authority. The Lord told them that the issue is not with the future but with today. The spirit of this subject is applicable not only to future glory but also to today. The Lord introduced the spirit that will be applicable from that day until the present. Here were two persons who wanted to sit on the throne to rule over others. The Lord showed them that among the Gentiles, there are those who are esteemed as rulers and great ones who lord it over them. Among the Gentiles there is the hunger for authority. Men like to be kings; they like to rule over others or to be great ones to control others. But it is not so among us. It is good if some among us seek for future glory, but such ones should not have the thought of lording it over God's children today. They should not have the thought of controlling or ruling others.

There is nothing wrong for man to want to sit on the Lord's right or left side. But there should not be any striving for supremacy among God's children. There should not be any thought of struggle for power or any intention of controlling others. If we do, we will fall into the same condition as that of the Gentiles. Nothing is more unsightly than a person who struggles to be an authority. It is the most ugly thing for a person to try to control others in an outward way. Ambition for authority or to be a great one is something that belongs to the Gentiles. We should drive this kind of spirit from the church. The Lord can only use those who know His cup and who are willing to be baptized with His baptism. If we drink His cup and take His baptism, authority will be ours spontaneously. This is the God-ordained way, the root of everything. If we do not take this way yet try to reach our destination, or if we do not have the root yet try to produce fruit, we are trying in vain. We must abound in our knowledge of God's will and must accept all the breakings so that the life within can be released. As far as our position before God is concerned, it is up to God's preparation. If anyone wants to climb above other children of God, or if he wants to take control and rule, I will say that such a one is a Gentile in reality. We must first drive out this Gentile spirit from among us. Among us, we should not tolerate the spirit of the Gentiles. We are after those whom God can use, not those who can rule over others. Such a Gentile spirit must be thoroughly purged from us before we can go down from this mountain to help others or handle business affairs.

The more a person wants to be an authority or a great one, the less we can entrust him with authority. God never grants authority to those who want to be His authority. The more Gentile spirit a person has, the less God can use him.

I hope none of us are politicians, manipulating, controlling, and hushing others, while allowing only ourselves to be the ones to issue the orders. We cannot do this. The more a person realizes his foibles, the more authority God will give to him. Since this is how the Lord selects men, this is the way we should take. We must never be a politician and must never play politics. We should never say, "If we do not give this man some position, he will rebel against us." We cannot deal with others this way. In God's house we can only take the spiritual way according to the spiritual principle; we cannot take the way of politicians. I hope that you will be faithful. You should be meek and pliable in your attitude, but you have to be faithful before the Lord. A man can only be used by God after he has prostrated himself before Him. When a man is standing tall, God can never use him.

In verses 42 and 43 the Lord said that the Gentiles have rulers and great men to rule over them, but "it is not so among you." I like the words *among you.* This means that there is a great difference between the Gentiles and the church in the matter of authority. If we are not careful in this matter, we will have no way to go on in the church. The Gentiles rule according to position, but the church serves according to its spiritual life. Once the church is contaminated with this Gentile practice, it is ruined. The church has to maintain a strict separating wall between it and the Gentiles. Among the Gentiles, one only sees power struggles. Among us, the more a person thinks that he is authority, the less he is qualified to be the authority. The more a person thinks he is qualified, the less he is qualified. We should maintain this attitude among us at all times.

WHOEVER WANTING TO BECOME GREAT SHALL BE THE SERVANT, AND WHOEVER WANTING TO BE FIRST SHALL BE THE SLAVE

The Lord uses the phrase *among you* three times. Today the Lord is establishing authority in the church. Those who are great in the church, that is, those who are established by the Lord as great ones, are actually the servants and slaves of all. Whoever wants to become great shall be the servant of all, and whoever wants to be the first shall be the slave of all. This is the authority in the church. Here we see the two great requirements for a man to be appointed as God's authority. First, there is the need to drink the cup—obedience to God's will absolutely—and to accept the baptism—acknowledgment of death for the release of life. Second, there should not be any ambition for power. One should only be a servant, a slave of all. On the one hand, one should have a spiritual basis; he should honor God's will as the central and highest thing among all things and should release the Lord's life. On the other hand, one has to be humble, which means having no interest in being the authority among the brothers and sisters and being satisfied with being a servant and a slave. God can only use such people as His authority. All those who are willing to be servants will be appointed by the Lord as the great ones, and they will be entrusted with authority. All those who are willing to be the slaves, that is, who have a heart to serve the brothers and sisters, will be appointed to be the first by the Lord. In other words, a man must have a spiritual foundation on the one hand, and have a proper attitude and view towards authority on the other hand. He must not have any craving for authority. Only men such as this can be God's authority.

I have laid out these two points in an honest way before you. If you do not possess the first point—a spiritual foundation, it will do you no good to possess the second—humility. You still will be useless even if you become very humble. When the Lord answered James and John, He first dealt with the first criterion. However, this does not mean that a person will be given the right or left side of the Lord after he has a spiritual foundation. The Lord said that it would be given to whoever God wills. After the first qualification, there is the need for the second condition, which is being a servant and a slave among the brothers and sisters. Those who fulfill these two conditions, who see themselves as unsuitable and incapable men, are the ones who are qualified to be the authority. The Lord is after those who consider themselves unqualified men, servants, and slaves. The Lord said that such ones can be made the great ones and the first. In order to be an authority, one has to drink the cup and take the baptism. Otherwise, all is in vain. But in addition to this, he has to be truly humble, considering himself worthy to be only a servant (not in word only, but in inward feeling). The Lord said that such a one can be great. We are afraid of the kind of humility that stays on one's lips only. Humility must be something that issues from the heart.

In order to be a deputy authority, we must fulfill the condition of spirituality as well as the condition of humility. The qualification of an authority is based on one's consciousness of his inability and unsuitability. One thing is sure: None of the persons that God used in the Old and New Testaments were proud. I can tell you frankly that as soon as a person becomes proud, God will put him aside. As a worker for over twenty years, I have never seen a proud man who was used by the Lord. Even if a man is just a little proud in private, his words will sooner or later expose him, because a person's words always disclose the hidden state of his heart. Even a humble person will be greatly surprised at the judgment seat. The surprise that awaits the proud, however, will surely be many times more than that of the humble! We must be conscious of our unprofitableness all the time, because God can only use the unprofitable slaves. We are not saying this to be polite. We honestly should feel that we are unprofitable slaves. We may have tended sheep or plowed the field, but when we come in from the field, we should still acknowledge that we are unprofitable slaves. We should always stand in the position of a slave (Luke 17:10). God never entrusts His authority to the self-confident and self-assured. We have to reject pride and learn humility and meekness. We should not speak for ourselves but should learn to know ourselves and to see things from God's viewpoint.

Finally the Lord said, "For even the Son of Man did not come to be served, but to serve and to give His life as a ransom for many" (Mark 10:45). The Lord did not come to be an authority but to serve. The less ambition a man has and the more he humbles himself before the Lord, the more useful he is in the eyes of the Lord. The more a man thinks highly of himself and the more he thinks he is different from others, the less he is useful in the hand of the Lord. The Lord took the form of a slave and became a slave to all. He never seized any authority; all of His authority came from God. The Lord was raised from a lowly place to the height. This is His principle. We should not try to seize any fleshly authority with fleshly hands. We should be the servants of all. Then when God commits certain responsibilities to us, we will learn to represent Him. The basis of authority is ministry, and there is ministry only where there is resurrection. When one has a ministry, he has a service, and when he has a service, he has authority. May the Lord deliver us from haughty thoughts.

A man who tries to usurp God's authority with his fleshly hands will suffer severe judgment! We have to fear authority as much as we fear hell fire. It is not an easy matter to represent God. It is too great a matter, something unfathomable to man, and something that we dare not touch with our own hands. We should take a straight course in obedience. Our way is the way of obedience, not the way of authority. It is a matter of being a servant, not a matter of being great. It is a matter of being a slave, not a matter of being the first. Moses and David were great authorities, yet neither of them built up their own authority. This should be the way of those who serve as authorities today. We should tremble with fear in our exercise of authority. May the Lord be merciful to us.

CHAPTER NINETEEN

THE NEED OF A DEPUTY AUTHORITY TO SANCTIFY HIMSELF

Scripture Reading: John 17:19

We have seen that spiritual authority depends on spiritual attainment. No authority is appointed by men. It is not even appointed by God alone. Please remember that authority is based on attainment on the one hand and on humility and obedience before God on the other hand. Today we will say something more about the need for a deputy authority to set himself apart from others. Although our Lord was sent from God and had uninterrupted fellowship with God, He said, "For their sake I sanctify Myself" (John 17:19). A deputy authority must therefore sanctify himself for others' sake.

THE LORD'S SANCTIFICATION OF HIMSELF

What does it mean that the Lord sanctified Himself? It means that the Lord refrained from doing many things, which were legitimate for Him to do, for the sake of the disciples. He could have done and said many things. He could have adopted many attitudes. He could have worn many different kinds of clothing and eaten many different kinds of food. For the sake of the disciples, however, He refrained from them. The Lord Jesus is the Son of God; He does not know sin. While He was on the earth, He had much more liberty than we have, and He could have done many more things than we. There are many things which we cannot do because we are the wrong person. There are many words we cannot speak because we are unclean persons. But such a problem did not exist with the Lord. He is holy. We are impatient; therefore, we need to learn to wait. But the Lord was never impatient; therefore, He did not need to wait. There are many restrictions which did not have to apply to Him, because He had no sin. Without the unclean ones being around Him, the Lord Jesus as a man could have had so much more liberty. Even when He was angry, His anger was holy and without sin. Yet He said that He sanctified Himself for the disciples' sake. He was willing to take many restrictions.

The Lord was not only holy before God; He was holy in Himself. As far as His own character is concerned, He is without sin. But while He moved among His disciples, He needed to sanctify Himself. For us to become holy we need to refrain from many things, but the Lord is holy in His very nature. This is why He can do so many more things than we can. It would be very wrong for anyone to say that he is good. But it is perfectly all right for the Lord to say that He is good. He can say many things that we cannot say, because there is no taint of sin in Him whatsoever. He has more freedom than we have. Yet He willingly subjected Himself to restrictions. The Lord is not only holy in Himself, He condescended to our holiness. Our holiness necessitates our setting ourselves apart from others and refraining from doing many things.

In addition to His own holiness, the Lord took our holiness upon Himself. This is why He sanctified Himself. The Lord willingly accepted restriction for our sake. Man speaks and judges by his own sinful standard. If the Lord had acted and spoken according to His own standard of holiness, man would have criticized Him according to his own sinful thoughts. This is why He willingly placed Himself under restrictions. We refrain from doing many things because of our sins, but the Lord refrained from doing many things and placed Himself under restrictions because of holiness. We do not do things because we should not do them. The Lord could have done them, yet He did not. He refrained from many things which He otherwise could have done for the sake of maintaining God's authority. He wanted to set Himself apart from the world. This is what it meant for the Lord to sanctify Himself.

THE LONELINESS OF AN AUTHORITY

In order for us to learn to be an authority, we must also learn to set ourselves apart from the brothers and sisters.

We need to refrain from many things which we otherwise could do or say. We should be separated in our speech and in our emotion. We may hold a certain attitude when we are by ourselves. But when we are with others, we have to set ourselves apart. We can only fellowship with the brothers and sisters to a certain extent. We cannot be flippant or frivolous. We need to give up our freedom and suffer loneliness. Loneliness is a mark of being an authority. All those who are frivolous among the brothers and sisters cannot be an authority. This is not pride. It merely means that for the sake of representing God's authority, we have to have certain limitations in our fellowship with the brothers and sisters. We cannot be too loose or easy-going. Sparrows fly in company, but the eagles fly alone. If we can only fly low and not suffer the loneliness of flying high, we are not qualified to be an authority. In order to be an authority, we have to be restricted and must separate ourselves. We cannot do what others can freely do. We cannot say what others can hastily say. We have to submit to the Spirit of the Lord. The Holy Spirit within us will teach us. This will make us lonely; it will strip us of excitement. We will no longer dare to joke around the brothers and sisters. This is the price that an authority has to pay. We must sanctify ourselves as the Lord Jesus did before we can be an authority.

As far as being a member in the Body is concerned, an authority has to be absolutely inconspicuous, being the same as the other brothers and sisters, in order to maintain the fellowship of the Body. However, in representing God, an authority has to be restricted by God and sanctified. He should be a pattern to the saints. But in acting as a member, he should coordinate and serve together with others, not setting himself apart as a special class.

AN AUTHORITY HAS TO BE RESTRICTED IN HIS EMOTION

Leviticus 10:1-7 records God's judgment on Nadab and Abihu. They were judged because they did not come under the authority of their father Aaron. Aaron had four sons, who served as priests in the sanctuary; they were anointed the same day that he was anointed. They were not supposed to

serve independently; rather, they were to help their father in
his service to God. They could not do anything by themselves.
But one day Nadab and Abihu offered up strange fire on their
own, without the command of their father. This brought in
God's judgment, and they were burned to death. Moses said,
"This is what Jehovah spoke, saying, I will be sanctified by
those who come near to Me" (v. 3). God wanted to point out
that those who draw near to Him cannot be loose. This
punishment was more severe and strict than His discipline
on the rest of His people.

Nadab and Abihu died on the same day. What should
Aaron have done? Before God he was the high priest; in his
house he was the head of his household. He played a double
role. Can a man be so dedicated to God's service that he can
ignore his sons? According to Jewish tradition, when a man
dies, his family has to dishevel their hair and tear their
garments. But Moses only ordered the corpses to be carried
out. Aaron and his sons were not allowed to dishevel their
hair or tear their garments.

Sorrow and grief over death are human affections; they
are normal. But here a servant of the Lord could not express
his sorrow or else he would die. This is a very sober matter.
The judgment that a servant of God can suffer is different
from the judgment that an ordinary Israelite can suffer. A
servant of God cannot do what an ordinary Israelite can do.
It is understandable and legitimate for a father to mourn
over his son or for a person to mourn over his own brother.
But those who have God's anointing oil upon them must
sanctify themselves. This is not a matter of sin but a matter
of sanctification. We cannot say that we can do many things
just because they are legitimate and not sinful. It is not a
matter of whether or not they are sinful, but whether we are
sanctified. It may be right for others to do them, but a servant
of God cannot because he must sanctify himself.

The opposite of sanctification is being common. To be
sanctified means that we cannot do what everybody else can
do. The Lord could not do what the disciples could do. An
authority cannot do what his brothers can do. A high priest
cannot even express his own emotion which he would

otherwise be entitled to express. If he becomes loose in this matter, he will die. The Israelites died because of sin, while the priests died because of the failure of separation. Among the children of Israel, those who kill die, but Aaron would die if he were to weep for his sons. What a difference this is! An authority must pay the price.

Aaron could not even leave the tabernacle. He could only let others bury the dead. The Israelites did not have to live in the tabernacle at all, yet Aaron and his sons could not even leave the door of the tabernacle. They had to carefully guard that which God had entrusted to them. The holy ointment has sanctified us and separated us from all our activities. We have to honor the ointment that God has given us. All of us have to go to God to deal with Him and to ask Him to separate us from others. The world and other brothers and sisters may maintain their family affections, but a deputy authority is set apart to maintain God's glory. He cannot seek for ease. He cannot hold on to his own feelings. He cannot rebel or be loose. He must instead exalt God for His glory.

A servant of God is one who has God's holy ointment upon him. He must sacrifice his own emotion and abandon his legitimate sentiments. This is the only way to become a deputy authority. Anyone who maintains God's authority must also reject his own feeling. One must be willing to pay any price, even to the extent of giving up his deepest affections, his filial sentiments, his friendships, and even his love. If he is entangled by these things, he cannot serve the Lord. God's requirements are strict. If a man does not give up his own affections, he cannot serve the Lord. God's servants are those with a distinction, while ordinary people are those without a distinction. God's servants must sanctify themselves for the sake of His people.

AN AUTHORITY MUST SANCTIFY HIMSELF
IN HIS LIVING AND HIS ENJOYMENT

Why did Nadab and Abihu offer up strange fire? According to Leviticus 10:9, God told Aaron, "Do not drink wine or strong drink, you or your sons with you, when you come into the tent of meeting." Many who are familiar with the Bible think that these two offered up strange fire after becoming drunk with wine. According to the record of verse 5, it is possible that they became naked in the sanctuary. This is why others came in and carried them in their tunics after they died. It is very easy for a drunken person to expose his body. The Israelites can take wine or strong drink, but a priest could not do the same. This is a matter of enjoyment. We cannot enjoy what others enjoy, and we cannot rejoice in what others rejoice in. (Wine signifies joy.) A servant of God has to be restricted. He has to separate the holy from the common, the clean from the unclean. It is right for us to maintain our fellowship in the Body with the brothers and sisters, but we cannot be loose, because we bear a special service. We cannot engage in anything that will induce us to cast off all restraints.

Leviticus 21 records God's specific requirement of sanctification on His serving priest:

(1) They cannot defile themselves by death, except for their relatives who are near to them. They have to sanctify themselves (vv. 1-4). This is the general requirement.

(2) One has to be sanctified in his attire and in the body (vv. 5-6). He cannot make any baldness on his head, and he cannot shave off the corners of his beard. (Egyptians did this when they worshipped the sun god.) Neither can they make any cuttings in their flesh. (Africans do this.)

(3) One has to be sanctified in marriage (vv. 7-9).

(4) The high priest is bound by a higher requirement: He cannot touch a dead body, not even when it is his father or mother (vv. 10-15). Therefore, the higher a servant of God stands, the higher God's requirements are. God pays attention to whether or not His servants are separated. The more a person is near to God, the higher God's requirements are upon him. The degree of our nearness to God becomes the degree of God's requirement on us. The more God entrusts Himself to a person, the more He requires of a person. God pays much attention to the sanctification of those who serve Him.

THE BASIS OF AUTHORITY BEING SEPARATION

Authority is based on separation. Without separation there is no authority. If you crave the company of others, you cannot be an authority. If your communication with others is unrestricted, you cannot be a deputy authority. The higher an authority stands, the greater is the separation. God is the highest authority. Therefore, He exercises the greatest separation. We all have to learn to separate ourselves from others in unholy things. The Lord Jesus could have acted as He willed, but He sanctified Himself for the disciples' sake. He separated Himself and stood on the side of holiness. We should willingly and gladly pursue after deeper separations—separation from unholiness. This does not mean that we should separate ourselves from God's children through self-proclaimed holiness. The more we are sanctified and the more we are restricted by God and bound under His authority, the more we can be an authority. Obedience cannot be maintained in the church if those who are in authority do not behave properly. If the issue of authority is not settled, there will always be confusion in the church.

Those who are in authority do not usurp authority. An authority is a servant of God. He must pay any price to shun excitement. He must climb high, he must not be afraid of loneliness, and he must be a sanctified person. May we be willing to pay the price to recover God's authority. This is the way the Lord is taking in the church today.

CHAPTER TWENTY

THE REQUIREMENTS OF
A DEPUTY AUTHORITY

Scripture Reading: Eph. 5:22, 25, 28, 33; 6:1, 4, 9; Psa. 82:1-2; 1 Tim. 4:12; 3:4-6; Titus 2:15; 1:6-8; 1 Pet. 1:21

God has appointed authorities in many places. In the family there are husbands, parents, and masters. Above us there are rulers and officers. In the church there are elders and workers. Each deputy authority has his own requirements. Today we will consider the requirements for these different deputy authorities.

THE REQUIREMENTS OF VARIOUS DEPUTY AUTHORITIES

Concerning Husbands

The Bible teaches the wife to submit to the husband and the husband to exercise authority. However, there are requirements which the husband has to fulfill. Ephesians 5 mentions three times that the husband has to love the wife. He has to love his wife as himself. Although there is such a thing as authority in the family, those who are in authority should fulfill God's requirements. The requirement of a husband as a deputy authority is to love his wife. There is a pattern for the husband's love for the wife—Christ's love for the church. Just as Christ loved the church, husbands should love their wives. The love that a husband has towards his wife should match that of Christ's love towards the church. In order for a husband to maintain his authority in representing God, he must love his wife.

Concerning Parents

Children should obey their parents. But as deputy authorities, parents also have their responsibilities and requirements. The Bible says that parents should not provoke their children to anger. Although parents have authority over their children, they have to learn to control themselves before God. They cannot say that since their children have been begotten and are being raised up by them, they can treat them at will. God created us, but He does not treat us at will. He gives everyone a free will. Hence, parents should not provoke their children to anger. Some people dare not do certain things before their friends, students, subordinates, or relatives, but they readily do them before their children without any hesitation at all. This is wrong. The greatest thing parents need to do is to exercise self-control. They have to control themselves through the Holy Spirit. Parents can deal with their children only to a certain extent. Their authority over their children is for the purpose of educating them only. They have to warn and nurture their children with the teaching of the Lord. There is no sense of domination or punishment here. A parent's heart should be for education, not for punishment.

Concerning Masters

Servants should be obedient to their masters. But there are requirements for those who are masters. A master should not intimidate his servants. He should not threaten them or be angry with them. God will not allow an authority to behave in an unrestrained way. He must fear God. Both the servant and the master have the same Master in the heavens. A master has to remember that he himself is under authority. Although others may be under him, he also is under authority, even God's authority. This is why he cannot be careless. The more a person knows authority, the less intimidating and threatening he will be. We have to learn to be meek and loving, always having a heart for perfecting others. This is a necessary attitude for one to be an authority. If a deputy authority only knows to threaten and judge others, he will come under God's judgment sooner or later. Therefore, a master must learn to walk with fear and trembling before God.

Concerning Rulers

We should submit to the authority of rulers and officers over us. We cannot find a teaching in the New Testament concerning how to be a ruler. God has given charge of the world to the unbelievers. He has not given it to the Christians. In the New Testament God gives no indication that Christians should be rulers in the world. But in the Old Testament there are cases of men serving as civil servants (Psa. 82). Of those in position and power, God requires righteousness, integrity, fairness, and compassion on the poor. This is the proper principle for those who are executing authority in public office. A man who is over others should not try to uphold his own standing; instead, he should do his utmost to uphold righteousness.

Concerning Elders

The elders are the authorities in the local church. All the brothers have to submit to the elders. Titus 1 speaks of basic qualifications of an elder—self-control and submission. A lawless person can never execute the law, and a rebellious person can never make others submissive. An elder must exercise strict self-control. A common trait among many people is the lack of discipline. Hence, in appointing elders, we have to select those who are particularly exercised in self-control. God appoints the elders to manage the church. As such, they must be submissive and must exercise self-control. They must set their hearts to be a pattern to all in everything. God never appoints a person who loves to be the first among others (like Diotrephes) to be an elder. The elders are the highest deputy authority in a local church. For this reason they must be men with self-control.

First Timothy 3:4-5 speaks of another basic qualification of an elder—he must be able to manage his own house. Managing one's house does not refer to managing one's parents or wife, but it refers mainly to managing one's children. An elder has to teach his children to walk soberly and to be obedient in all things. A man must first be a good father before he can be an elder. He must first be an authority at home before he can be an elder in the church.

An elder must not be an arrogant person. If a person becomes proud as soon as he assumes authority, he is not qualified to be an elder. An elder in a local church should feel as if he has no authority at all. If an elder is always conscious of his authority, he is not qualified to be an elder or to handle the affairs of the church. Only the foolish and the narrow-minded are proud. Such ones cannot stand the temptation of God's glory, and they cannot bear God's commission and assignment. Once such ones are entrusted with something, they fall into a snare. This is why a new convert cannot be an overseer (1 Tim. 3:6—in Greek this word means a novice in a trade. For example, among carpenters there are masters who have been in the trade for decades, and there are novices who have barely learned to handle a hammer.), lest he be blinded with pride and fall into the judgment suffered by the devil.

Concerning the Lord's Workers

Titus 2:15 describes the requirements of a deputy authority in the Lord's work. Titus was not an elder in the church, but a worker of the Lord, serving in the capacity of an apostle. Paul charged Titus to exhort men. He should not only speak in public but also exhort men one by one. He should convict men with all authority. At the same time, he should not let others despise him in words and deeds. In order for others not to despise us, we have to sanctify ourselves. If we are the same as others in many things, and if we are loose, careless, and unchecked in our daily life, others will despise us. We must not be indulgent in anything. Only then will others respect us and honor us as an authority and a representative of God. This is what Paul told Timothy (1 Tim. 4:12). Although a worker should not seek after human glory or honor, he should neither be despised to the point of losing his sanctified stature.

In the entire New Testament, Paul wrote only two books which were directed toward young co-workers. They are 1 Timothy and Titus. In these two books Paul often said that a worker should not dishonor himself but should be a pattern in everything. Anything that leads to contempt should be avoided; one should refuse such things. There is a price to pay in being an authority. One has to separate himself from others. He has to be able to live alone. A pattern must be different from others; he must sanctify himself. If he is the same as the others, he is no longer a pattern. We should not uplift ourselves, but at the same time we should not make others despise us. We should always sanctify ourselves and should not jest lightly. We have to learn to separate ourselves in the Lord. A worker should not be arrogant, but neither should he give reason for others to despise him. Once a worker becomes too common, he is disqualified from his work. Once he becomes too common, his usefulness is gone, and his authority is lost.

A worker must also keep his standing and maintain God's authority. Authority manifests itself in separation and distinction. The main thing about a representative authority is that he represents God, and being an authority has everything to do with being a pattern. This is a very serious matter. A deputy authority is one who "represents" authority, not one who "exercises" authority.

HOW GOD DEALS WITH THE MISTAKES OF THE DEPUTY AUTHORITY

Numbers 30:13 tells us how God upholds His appointed deputy authority. It says that a husband can establish the vow his wife vows, or make it void. On the one hand, God tells the wife to submit to the husband. On the other hand, He upholds the authority of the husband. Even if the husband voids both the vow and the oath of the wife, she has to submit, and it is not reckoned to her as a sin if she breaks them. If the husband voids the vow of the wife, he will have to bear his wife's iniquity. We who are deputy authorities may propose something. Those who are under us should submit to authority. They may be wrong, but the sin is not reckoned upon them. However, we who make the proposal will have to bear their iniquity. Therefore, we should never propose or suggest anything rashly, because we will have to bear the consequence of it. The most dangerous thing is to be a counselor of the church and to propose something lightly. We can find no clearer picture of man's requirement to submit to deputy authority in the Bible than in Numbers 30. There we see God asking man to submit to deputy authority unconditionally. In the same way, there is no clearer picture of the serious responsibility that an authority bears before God than in Numbers 30. The more proposals a deputy authority makes, the more trouble he is asking for himself, and the more he will invite God's judgment.

We have to learn to not control others' lives presumptuously. We should not subject others to our own ideas. Before we have the full assurance, we should not take the burden of others upon ourselves. Only a broken and pliable man will be free from iniquity before God. A hard and opinionated man will bear much iniquity before God. The Body life is the basis of guidance in the church. We have to live in the Body life, to fellowship with the Lord, and to fellowship with the brothers and sisters. We should not be individualistic in our decisions, and we should not be so self-assured. The more we present our decision to the church and the more we fellowship with the members, the more assurance we will have. We should never bear the name of the Body while occupying ourselves with activities of the flesh. If we do, we should expect nothing except the bearing of our own iniquity. We should wait before the Lord, understand His will, and be open to others. We should not speak before we are taught or relate things to others before we see them ourselves. If we do, we will lay up iniquity for ourselves. A deputy authority must be meek and humble. This will save him from getting into trouble. Otherwise, God will have strong words for him because he will bear the iniquity of others. This is a sober matter.